MIXED COMPANY

GU00702822

MIXED COMPANY

The Bible Inspires

James Crichton

THE SAINT ANDREW PRESS: EDINBURGH

First published in 1988 by
THE SAINT ANDREW PRESS
121 George Street, Edinburgh EH2 4YN

Copyright © James Crichton 1988
ISBN 0 7152 0626 5

All rights reserved. No part of this publication may be reproduced or
transmitted in any form or by any means, electronic or mechanical,
including photocopy, recording, or information storage and retrieval
system, without permission in writing from the publisher. This book is
sold subject to the condition that it shall not, by way of trade or
otherwise, be lent, resold, hired out or otherwise circulated without the
publisher's prior consent.

British Library Cataloguing in Publication Data

Crichton, James 1944–
Mixed company.
1. Christians. Biographies
I. Title
209′.2′2

ISBN 0–7152–0626–5

Typeset by J&L Composition Ltd, Filey, North Yorkshire
Printed by Bell and Bain Ltd, Glasgow

Contents

Preface

In these pages you will meet a number of men and women; fifty seven, to be precise. Some of them you will already know. Others, perhaps, you will be meeting for the first time. They are a very mixed group — statesmen and soldiers, poets and boxers, explorers and inventors — but they all have one thing in common. At some point in their lives a passage in the Bible spoke to them and nothing was ever quite the same again.

For some, these were the words that first made them think about God and his place in their lives. For others, these were the words that, after long searching, finally brought them peace. Again, for others, these were the words that helped them meet a particular crisis. For others, these were the words that inspired their whole working life. But in each case — and each case is different — something happened.

This does not mean that there was no other Scripture that mattered to them. It does not mean that this was the only time they felt that God had something to tell them. It does mean that in every case recorded here, with each of these passages, God was heard to speak.

Some of the passages are well-known. Others may occasion some surprise. Through them all God spoke.

And they listened. Some were happy to listen. Others were not. But they did listen. And, because they listened, things happened. Things still do — whenever people listen to the Word.

James Crichton, 1988

Sir James Young Simpson
(1811–1870)

Genesis 2:21

So the Lord God caused a deep sleep to fall upon the man, and while he slept took one of his ribs and closed up its place with flesh;

The house in Edinburgh's Queen Street is still pointed out. An inscription by the front door tells us that it was here, in the dining room of Number 52, that one of the great medical discoveries of the age was made. Here, one night in the autumn of 1847, Professor Simpson and his colleagues Keith and Duncan found out the anaesthetic qualities of chloroform.

Since his earliest days as a medical student James Simpson had been searching for something that would relieve patients' pain. He was particularly anxious to help the plight of women in childbirth. He had experimented with hypnotism, but with little success. Then early in 1846 he heard about the use of ether in America. He was among the first in Europe to try it. However, while intensely grateful for the benefits it brought, he soon realised that there were difficulties and even dangers. He wanted something quicker, safer, easier to handle, and less unpleasant.

Thus it was that, late at night, his house in Queen Street became the scene of eager experiment. Simpson decided that the best way to test a gas was to inhale it himself. Then he would really know if it worked!

The bottle of chloroform had been sitting on his table for some days. An old college friend, now a chemist in Liverpool — David Waldie — had first mentioned its possibilities. Simpson had had a bottle made up by his local chemist, but had not felt very confident about it and so he had left it on one side. Until this night in November. Having tried other substances without any results, Simpson brought over the bottle. He and his assistants each took a tumbler ... and within moments all three were lying on the floor. Coming round, they tried again, being joined in their experiments by a niece who had been wakened by their noise. Other guests were brought in to see the effects. There was no doubt about it, chloroform worked.

On 8 November 1847 Simpson used chloroform for the first time in a delivery. The child was later photographed and Simpson kept her picture above his desk. He called her 'St Anaesthesia'. It was first used in surgery two days later.

Yet the real battle was only beginning. The medical world had still to be convinced. Oh yes, they could see it worked. But, the question was, should it be allowed? Was it right to deaden pain? In particular, they asked, was it right to use anaesthetics in childbirth? Did not the Bible say, 'in sorrow thou shalt bring forth children' (Gen 3:16)? There were, of course, other more strictly medical objections — being unable to answer questions might put the mother at risk — but the major argument was the ethical one.

Simpson had to answer this attack. Otherwise, chloroform and even ether would not be allowed by other doctors. Simpson was not afraid to argue his case. First, he took up the text quoted by his critics and argued that they were not being true to the meaning of the original Hebrew which, he said, did not refer to physical pain at all.

Then he produced his own evidence. He turned to Genesis 2:21. This showed, he said, that God used an 'anaesthetic'. This was surely the first operation in history, he argued, and it demonstrated that God wished to spare his creatures pain. Hence the use of anaesthetics was in perfect harmony with the mind of the Creator.

Simpson went on to issue a pamphlet on the religious aspect of the controversy. It became his most famous publication. He headed it with quotations from 1 Timothy 4:4 and James 4:17, and in it he forcefully argued that Christ came to bring mercy and so any discovery that would alleviate suffering was good. This pamphlet, following on his highly publicised argument from Genesis 2, helped decide the issue ... although Queen Victoria played her part when she had chloroform during the birth of her next child.

The ethical and religious aspects of the question were crucial, and Simpson's success as an advocate was almost as important as the discovery itself. It is interesting to note that these matters of religion were debated by medical men. Simpson, for his part, had no difficulty in assembling his biblical evidence and he was guilty of no hypocrisy in its use. From his early days as a baker's son in Bathgate he had been actively involved in the life of the Church and during his time in Edinburgh he was a regular attender.

Yet despite his religious upbringing, his attendance at church and his deep respect for certain ministers, there came a time when Simpson found his faith shaken. Always acutely interested in discovery of all kinds, he had followed the evolution debate with keen attention and he became genuinely worried. He could not help wondering if it was really possible to accept the findings of scientific research and still believe in the Bible.

It was the illness, the fatal illness, of his third son, Jamie, that helped him. The lad was only 15 and his bearing under sickness and pain and the example of his simple faith convinced Simpson of the reality of religion.

As always he was not the man to keep his discoveries to himself. In February 1862 he gave his first talk on religion. He identified himself closely with the work of the Carrubber's Close Mission, and often presided at meetings. And he continued to work with all his customary energy until, at the age of 59, he passed away after a brief illness.

He did many things in his life; characteristically he said, 'I have done some work. I wish I had been busier.' He will be remembered for his pioneer work in various fields, and particularly for introducing chloroform and winning its acceptance. Yet for Simpson himself there was, he said, a still greater discovery: when 'I found that I have a Saviour.'

Alexander Shields
(1660–1700)

Genesis 49:21

> Naph'tali is a hind let loose,
> that bears comely fawns.

It is often said that Alexander Duff was the first Church of Scotland missionary to be sent overseas. That is not so. In 1699 two ministers and two probationers were set apart to accompany the members of the second Darien expedition. While they were under instructions to form a presbytery at Darien with the ministers who had gone with the first expedition, and while they were to minister to the settlers, they were also sent with the express intent 'to labour among the natives for their instruction and conversion'. This was the first missionary enterprise of the Church of Scotland.

Those taking part in the venture were, of necessity, unusual men. Their natural leader was the 39-year-old Alexander Shields. He sailed from the Clyde prepared for the worst, while hoping for the best. He had already experienced a full share of hardship and danger.

He was first arrested in London. That was back in 1685 when Shields, already on the Fugitives' Roll for his Covenanting sympathies, was preaching to a small congregation in Cheapside. He remembered that day well. He had been preaching on his favourite text — 'Naphtali is a hind let loose' — when the soldiers arrived. After some time in Newgate prison, they took him back to Scotland.

The authorities were determined to use Shields for propaganda purposes. So they spent some time and much ingenuity in persuading him to a partial recantation. Eventually they got him to disown the Covenanter statement known as the Apologetic Declaration. That is, they got him to disown part of it. They then rewarded Shields by sending him to prison on the Bass Rock.

While on the rock Shields began to work out his position. He started to write a treatise on 'human and Christian liberty'. He was to call this book *A Hind Let Loose*. At this point there was a change in government policy and the Bass prisoners were brought to Edinburgh and held in the Tolbooth, from where Shields made a daring escape dressed as a woman. They never caught him again.

Shields made his peace with the Covenanters, admitting that he had been wrong to disown their struggle, and completely identifying himself with their cause. Shields had a price on his head but, despite all efforts, he kept one step ahead of the dragoons. There were several close escapes, as at Tinkhorn Hill in Ayrshire, but Shields maintained his freedom. He also managed to get over to Holland where he saw into print a number of Covenanter pieces, including his own *A Hind Let Loose*. The book was of course banned.

The arrival of William of Orange and the overthrow of the Stuarts changed everything. Shields was among those who argued that the Covenanters, split as they were in different factions, should unite behind William and rejoin the national Church. Not everyone agreed. Shields suited his action to his words, however, and became a chaplain with the newly created Cameronian regiment. He missed the Battle of Dunkeld which effectively secured William's hold on Scotland. But there were to be other battles.

He served with the regiment on the continent (1691–1695). A weary business it proved, disease being at least as great a danger as the enemy. The regiment played a notable part in the campaigns with Angus' Regiment (the Cameronians) and Shields stayed with them until near the end when he was summoned home by the General Assembly.

In 1697 he became minister at St Andrews. He later called his time there 'the longest and pleasantest time of rest that I ever had', but that only reminds us of how grim the other times had been. There were problems enough at St Andrews where a serious food shortage, following on a bad harvest, called for all his leadership skills. There were the starving poor to be fed, and the selfish rich to be persuaded to feed them. Shields got the job done. One of the freedoms he did not believe in was the freedom to let other folk starve.

So they sent him to Darien, accompanied by his brother Michael as his secretary. His experiences of army service had given him some idea of what to expect. But it was worse than he had ever imagined.

Before the convoy had left Rothesay illness broke out. There was no proper medicine and both the food and the water were rotten. 'Tedious and miserable' was Shields summary of the voyage.

Their arrival at Darien deepened the gloom. Instead of a flourishing colony they found ruined huts and overgrown fields with a handful of survivors. In the circumstances no one was very much interested in what the ministers had to say. If they wanted a church they could build it themselves.

So Shields decided to take up the other aspect of their work and organised a journey inland to meet the Indians. In fact the Indians were friendly and showed great kindness to the little party of missionaries. The only trouble, naturally, was that they could not understand English, nor could the Scots speak their language and there were no interpreters. To make matters worse the missionary party then managed to get lost and only reached their base with great difficulty. Shields was utterly exhausted.

With things going from bad to worse, the colony was attacked by the Spanish. Despite some initial success and considerable bravery it soon became clear that their position was hopeless. They surrendered. Shields intervened in an effort to protect those Indians who had fought with them against the Spanish but it was his last effort to influence events.

The survivors finally limped into Jamaica. Brother Michael had died, and Alexander Shields himself fell ill. He had been able to preach only once at Port Royal since their arrival in Jamaica. Worn out and disappointed, he quickly got worse and died. A Scotswoman, Miss Isabel Murray, saw that he was properly buried.

All his life Alexander Shields had fought for freedom. He had been content to suffer, too. He found his inspiration in the Bible and, in particular, the hope that the hind of Christian truth would one day be let loose.

F W Boreham
(1871–1959)

1 Samuel 7:12
Then Samuel took a stone and set it up between Mizpah and Jesh'anah, and called its name Ebene'zer; for he said, 'Hitherto the Lord has helped us.'

'This,' said the Moderator, 'is the man whose name is on all our lips, whose books are on all our shelves, and whose illustrations are in all our sermons.' After such an introduction it is not surprising to learn that the guest went on to speak for three quarters of an hour and enjoyed himself immensely.

The scene was the Assembly Hall in Edinburgh, the occasion the 1936 General Assembly of the Church of Scotland; the Moderator was Professor Daniel Lamont, and the guest speaker thus introduced was F W Boreham.

In some ways it was a surprising scene. Boreham, after all, was a Baptist not a Presbyterian, and he was an Englishman who had made his name in New Zealand and Australia. But then, Boreham's life was full of surprises.

He had no idea of becoming a minister when as a young man he went to work in an office in London. And when, to his own surprise, the call to service did come, he felt sure that he was meant to be a missionary. He wanted to be sent to China. However, the effects of an accident — suffered in early manhood — meant that he really wasn't able for the rough and tumble of the mission field. It was Dr Hudson Taylor who pointed this out to Boreham over tea.

So what was left? Boreham did not need to look far for an answer. There was a job to be done right there in London. He decided to do what he could. His efforts as a street preacher were to have surprising results.

Boreham was befriended by James Douglas, a well-known Baptist preacher. It was Douglas who persuaded him to think of the full-time ministry and, largely through Douglas' influence, he was accepted for training by Spurgeon's College. Boreham had happy memories of his student days, hearing many of the notable preachers of the time, making many true friends, and — to his surprise — meeting his future wife.

A further surprise was New Zealand. According to Boreham's own story, it was really a very strange business. One day a college pal asked him where he wanted to go when he left college. Boreham had not given the matter much thought — he thought he would be at college for another year at least — but he immediately replied, 'I would go to New Zealand.' The next day he was called into Professor Marchant's room, and invited to go to New Zealand to take up the new work at a place called Mosgiel. He accepted.

Boreham became a writer in a way that surprised himself. The small town of Mosgiel had its own newspaper. It occurred to Boreham that people who would not or could not come to church read the paper. He therefore asked if some religious articles could be carried, and he was given two columns in the Saturday edition.

Then he got space in one of the large Dunedin dailies ... because he missed a train. Acting on impulse, and completely out of character, he went into the office, asked to see the editor, and rather diffidently offered himself as a writer — and found himself writing the leading article.

After that came the books. There were dozens of titles. All were popular, but the most popular came from a series of sermons; a series that had a most unusual beginning. Boreham was on the point of initiating another series of sermons, planned to run on a fortnightly basis, when he thought that he should say something on the other Sundays. And there and then, right in the pulpit, he decided to preach a series on the great texts of the Bible and the way they had made history. He had been reading Luther's life and he announced he would start with Luther's text.

From that accidental beginning, there grew a whole series of sermons and before long they appeared in print as *A Bunch of Everlastings*. Boreham would often say how much he himself benefited from this series; reading up the lives of famous Christians, meeting them afresh, his research brought a zest to his own ministry. And he saw again how the Bible speaks to men.

That, however, was a lesson he had learned long before. He first learned this truth from his mother. The family had been going through a rough time. Frank was too young to appreciate the problem but he could tell that something was wrong. He had never known his father to be so worried nor his mother to be so upset. Then one day everything changed. He did not know what had happened but something most certainly had. The only thing different that he could see was that there was a new piece of paper framed and hung on the wall. The paper carried these words: 'Hitherto the Lord has helped us.'

He got the story from his mother. She herself had put the text on the wall. It had caught her eye the day before. That had been an awful day, she said, and she had been pacing aimlessly up and down the room when suddenly she saw this text on an almanac. And it was as if someone was speaking to her. She sat down and cried. And that was it. Now she knew they would get through. They were not alone. The Lord was still there, as he always had been, and would be.

Frank Boreham never forgot his mother's story. It made him realise that God did care, and that God did speak. Later on he would help others learn the same lesson.

William 'Bendigo' Thompson
(1811–1880)

1 Samuel 17

Now the Philistines gathered their armies for battle; and they were gathered at Socoh, which belongs to Judah, and encamped between Socoh and Aze'kah, in E'phes-dam'mim. ²And Saul and the men of Israel were gathered, and encamped in the valley of Elah, and drew up in line of battle against the Philistines. ³And the Philistines stood on the mountain on the one side, and Israel stood on the mountain on the other side, with a valley between them. ⁴And there came out from the camp of the Philistines a champion named Goliath, of Gath, whose height was six cubits and a span. ⁵He had a helmet of bronze on his head, and he was armed with a coat of mail, and the weight of the coat was five thousand shekels of bronze. ⁶And he had greaves of bronze upon his legs, and a javelin of bronze slung between his shoulders. ⁷And the shaft of his spear was like a weaver's beam, and his spear's head weighed six hundred shekels of iron; and his shield-bearer went before him. ⁸He stood and shouted to the ranks of Israel, "Why have you come out to draw up for battle? Am I not a Philistine, and are you not servants of Saul? Choose a man for yourselves, and let him come down to me. ⁹If he is able to fight with me and kill me, then we will be your servants; but if I prevail against him and kill him, then you shall be our servants and serve us." ¹⁰And the Philistine said, "I defy the ranks of Israel this day; give me a man, that we may fight together." ¹¹When Saul and all Israel heard these words of the Philistine, they were dismayed and greatly afraid.

¹²Now David was the son of an Eph'rathite of Bethlehem in Judah, named Jesse, who had eight sons. In the days of Saul the man was already old and advanced in years. ¹³The three eldest sons of Jesse had followed Saul to the battle; and the names of his three sons who went to the battle were Eli'ab the first-born, and next to him Abin'adab, and the third Shammah. ¹⁴David was the youngest; the three eldest followed Saul, ¹⁵ but David went back and forth from Saul to feed his father's sheep at Bethlehem. ¹⁶For forty days the Philistine came forward and took his stand, morning and evening.

¹⁷And Jesse said to David his son, "Take for your brothers an ephah of this parched grain, and these ten loaves, and carry them quickly to the camp to your brothers; ¹⁸also take these ten cheeses to

the commander of their thousand. See how your brothers fare, and bring some token from them."

[19]Now Saul, and they, and all the men of Israel, were in the valley of Elah, fighting with the Philistines. [20]And David rose early in the morning, and left the sheep with a keeper, and took the provisions, and went, as Jesse had commanded him; and he came to the encampment as the host was going forth to the battle line, shouting the war cry. [21]And Israel and the Philistines drew up for battle, army against army. [22]And David left the things in charge of the keeper of the baggage, and ran to the ranks, and went and greeted his brothers. [23]As he talked with them, behold, the champion, the Philistine of Gath, Goliath by name, came up out of the ranks of the Philistines, and spoke the same words as before. And David heard him.

[24]All the men of Israel, when they saw the man, fled from him, and were much afraid. [25]And the men of Israel said, "Have you seen this man who has come up? Surely he has come up to defy Israel; and the man who kills him, the king will enrich with great riches, and will give him his daughter, and make his father's house free in Israel." [26]And David said to the men who stood by him, "What shall be done for the man who kills this Philistine, and takes away the reproach from Israel? For who is this uncircumcised Philistine, that he should defy the armies of the living God?" [27]And the people answered him in the same way, "So shall it be done to the man who kills him."

[28]Now Eli'ab his eldest brother heard when he spoke to the men; and Eli'ab's anger was kindled against David, and he said, "Why have you come down? And with whom have you left those few sheep in the wilderness? I know your presumption, and the evil of your heart; for you have come down to see the battle." [29]And David said, "What have I done now? Was it not but a word?" [30]And he turned away from him toward another, and spoke in the same way; and the people answered him again as before.

[31]When the words which David spoke were heard, they repeated them before Saul; and he sent for him. [32]And David said to Saul, "Let no man's heart fail because of him; your servant will go and fight with this Philistine." [33]And Saul said to David, "You are not able to go against this Philistine to fight with him; for you are but a youth, and he has been a man of war from his youth." [34]But David said to Saul, "Your servant used to keep sheep for his father; and when there came a lion, or a bear, and took a lamb from the flock, [35]I went after him and smote him and delivered it out of his mouth; and if he arose against me, I caught him by his beard, and smote him and killed him. [36]Your servant has killed both lions and bears; and this uncircumcised Philistine shall be like one of them, seeing he has

defied the armies of the living God." ³⁷And David said, "The
LORD who delivered me from the paw of the lion and from the paw of
the bear, will deliver me from the hand of this Philistine." And Saul
said to David, "Go, and the LORD be with you!" ³⁸Then Saul clothed
David with his armour; he put a helmet of bronze on his head, and
clothed him with a coat of mail. ³⁹And David girded his sword over
his armour, and he tried in vain to go, for he was not used to them.
Then David said to Saul, "I cannot go with these; for I am not used
to them." And David put them off. ⁴⁰Then he took his staff in his
hand, and chose five smooth stones from the brook, and put them in
his shepherd's bag or wallet; his sling was in his hand, and he drew
near to the Philistine.

⁴¹And the Philistine came on and drew near to David, with
his shield-bearer in front of him. ⁴²And when the Philistine looked,
and saw David, he disdained him; for he was but a youth, ruddy
and comely in appearance. ⁴³And the Philistine said to David,
"Am I a dog, that you come to me with sticks?" And the Philistine
cursed David by his gods. ⁴⁴The Philistine said to David, "Come
to me, and I will give your flesh to the birds of the air and to the
beasts of the field." ⁴⁵Then David said to the Philistine, "You
come to me with a sword and with a spear and with a javelin; but
I come to you in the name of the LORD of hosts, the God of the
armies of Israel, whom you have defied. ⁴⁶This day the LORD will
deliver you into my hand, and I will strike you down, and cut off
your head; and I will give the dead bodies of the host of the
Philistines this day to the birds of the air and to the wild beasts of the
earth; that all the earth may know that there is a God in Israel, ⁴⁷and
that all this assembly may know that the LORD saves not with sword
and spear; for the battle is the LORD and he will give you into our
hand."

⁴⁸When the Philistine arose and came and drew near to meet
David, David ran quickly toward the battle line to meet the Philistine.
⁴⁹And David put his hand in his bag and took out a stone, and slung
it, and struck the Philistine on his forehead; the stone sank into his
forehead, and he fell on his face to the ground.

⁵⁰So David prevailed over the Philistine with a sling and with a
stone, and struck the Philistine, and killed him; there was no sword
in the hand of David. ⁵¹Then David ran and stood over the Philistine,
and took his sword and drew it out of its sheath, and killed him,
and cut off his head with it. When the Philistines saw that their
champion was dead, they fled. ⁵²And the men of Israel and Judah
rose with a shout and pursued the Philistines as far as Gath and the
gates of Ekron, so that the wounded Philistines fell on the way from
Sha-araim as far as Gath and Ekron. ⁵³And the Israelites came back
from chasing the Philistines, and they plundered their camp. ⁵⁴And

David took the head of the Philistine and brought it to Jerusalem; but he put his armour in his tent.
[55]When Saul saw David go forth against the Philistine, he said to Abner, the commander of the army, "Abner, whose son is this youth?" And Abner said, "As your soul lives, O king, I cannot tell." [56]And the king said, "Inquire whose son the stripling is." [57]And as David returned from the slaughter of the Philistine, Abner tok him, and brought him before Saul with the head of the Philistine in his hand. [58]And Saul said to him, "Whose son are you, young man?" And David answered, "I am the son of your servant Jesse the Bethlemite."

> You didn't know of Bendigo! Well, that knocks me out!
> Who's your board school teacher? What's he been about?
> Chock-a-block with fairy tales . . . full of useless cram,
> And never heard o' Bendigo, the pride of Nottingham!

They named a racehorse after him. And a town in Australia. Conan Doyle wrote a poem about him, the one they called Bendigo.

Of course, that wasn't his real name. He was born in Nottingham in October 1811. He was then plain William Thompson. The Bendigo came from his being the last born of triplets. His father's family were solid, working folk, active in Dissenting circles. Hence the biblical allusion to Shadrach, Mesach, and Abednego. Abednego was soon simplified to Bendigo and sometimes to Bendy.

When he was 15 his father died and young Bendigo spent some time in the workhouse. This he never forgot. It was largely from a desire to protect his mother from a similar fate that he took up boxing. However, he would have been the first to admit that he enjoyed his work! A natural sportsman, he showed considerable aptitude for the rough bare-knuckle game, and after some instruction from local 'professors', he set out on his chosen career at the age of 16.

During his early years he built up a large local following. They in turn earned themselves a place in social history as the first travelling supporters and, by all accounts, these 'Nottingham Lambs' made sure their man got fair play — and sometimes a bit more.

Bendigo had 21 official contests and claimed the British championship twice. His greatest rival was Ben Caunt. He stood a good five inches taller than Bendigo and was the heavier man by three stones. They fought three times. Bendigo won the first on a foul. Caunt won the second: on a foul. Bendigo won the third: on a foul. It was that kind of rivalry.

Eventually Bendigo retired after coming back one more time to defend his title just to please his mother. That's when the trouble started. With little to do the old champion took to drinking heavily. He also took to politics, leading his 'Lambs' into action at election time. Finally he was arrested and sent down for two months.

A sermon he heard in jail started him thinking. It was based on the story of David and Goliath. Bendigo was caught up in the excitement of the narrative and when the giant fell he cried out, 'Bravo!' The thing was, it reminded him of his own fights with the giant Ben Caunt. The story had aroused more than a passing interest. Having found himself in one chapter he began to wonder if there were other things in the Bible that might also parallel his own experience. The Bible comes alive when we start to see ourselves in its pages, when we begin to say, 'But this is me! This is how I feel! This is exactly what I've been asking!'

Bendigo wanted to find some answers. And the right man appeared at the right time. This was Dick Weaver, a collier turned evangelist, known with good reason as 'Dauntless Dick'. Bendigo went to hear him preach. He went back again to hear more. Going home after one of Dick's sermons he knelt down in a field and gave his life to a new master.

Bendigo was never one to be idle. He soon felt that he himself had something to say, an experience to share. There was, however, a problem: he had never really learned to read or write. So he had to learn his Bible and his theology by heart. He had his own way of putting things too, and — as Conan Doyle's poem goes on to relate — he had his own way of dealing with hecklers.

Inevitably his fame drew crowds. Many were openly scornful; others were less than certain about his sincerity. Once in Oxford Street he met an old backer. 'I am now fighting Satan,' said Bendigo in answer to a question, 'and' he added, 'the victory shall be mine.' 'I hope so,' replied his former backer, 'but pray fight him more fairly than you fought Ben Caunt, or I may change my side.' 'Sir,' said Bendigo, 'you backed me against Ben Caunt and I won your money. So you've no cause to complain. I beat Caunt and I mean to beat the devil. So you had better back me again.'

Bendigo, it is sometimes said, occasionally fell from grace. But if he did feel the pull of his old habits he knew he had found a better way. And in this fight, too, he got back up and won through. As he once said, 'I was never a coward in the devil's cause, and I do not mean to be a coward in Christ's cause.' Nor was he. He had won cups and belts as a sportsman, but now he would say, 'There's a crown being prepared for old Bendigo that will never fade.'

Lady Grisell Baillie
(1822–1891)

2 Samuel 1:23

> Saul and Jonathan, beloved and
> lovely!
> In life and in death they were not
> divided;
> they were swifter than eagles,
> they were stronger than lions.

This chapter title may be misleading; it mentions one name only: that of Lady Grisell. Yet the whole point of the text is that we are to remember how close two people were. And they were close, these two. So while it is Lady Grisell who is the more famous, and justly so, her brother Robert should not be forgotten. When the marble shield was placed in the nave of Bowden Church — 'a tribute from many to whom their memory is sacred' — brother and sister were together. That is how they were remembered by those who knew them best, 'lovely and pleasant in their lives, and in their death not divided'.

There were 11 children in the family. It was a happy family, growing up at Mellerstain, with a good kind man for a father and a beautiful and gentle lady for a mother. Grisell inherited her mother's looks and nature, together with her father's quiet good humour and kindness. She got on well with all her brothers and sisters, but as the years passed something happened that drew her and Robert still closer.

Grisell was 25 when, in her own words, 'The strong hand of the Almighty was stretched forth for my salvation.' Like the rest of the family, she had always gone to church but now her faith deepened and matured. Her brother, a major in the army and away from home, went through a similar experience a year or so later. This caused him to resign his commission, much as he had loved army life, and brought him home. From then on, writes Grisell, they became constant companions and 'There was never a cloud between us.'

They were then living at Eildon Hall and Robert and Grisell soon established a daily routine. They met over breakfast at 8.30 am with the major invariably in buoyant good spirits. There was nothing gloomy about their religion. At 9.00 am the bell was rung and everyone gathered for family worship. Grisell would then read to her brother while he prayed. In the afternoon the two would usually go for a walk and they would talk over the readings. When they came in Robert would again pray. There would be more prayers at dinner and, always, last thing at night.

Grisell was also busy at home. The father had died and her mother grew weaker. Grisell was by now the only daughter at home and for seven years she stayed by her mother's side, a cheerfully devoted companion.

However, none of this explains why so many people were eager to commemorate the lives of Grisell and her brother. Yet the explanation is simple. Their piety was genuine and so it led them both to involve themselves in helping others. This took many forms.

For example, after they moved to Dryburgh Abbey, Grisell decided to rebuild the bridge over the Tweed. The original bridge had been all but destroyed in the great storm of June 1840. True, there was a ferry, but it was slow and sometimes dangerous. There was a need for a bridge. Everyone had been saying so for over 30 years. But, characteristically, Grisell saw the need and met it. While others looked at the problem, she solved it, meeting the entire costs herself.

Something similar happened in the village of Newtown St Boswells. The villagers lacked a decent water supply and Grisell made sure they got one. In addition, she felt that the village needed a community centre. She herself had held meetings for the mothers of the district and realised the advantages a proper meeting place would bring. So she built it. She also made sure that books and magazines were supplied so that the locals got the chance to keep up their reading.

Yet even this does not explain their popularity. It was never enough just to spend money. Brother and sister got involved personally. They both taught in the Sunday School at Bowden, leaving home at 9.30 am and not returning until 3.00 pm. Then Grisell would have her meetings in the evening. For 34 years Robert was an elder and faithfully visited the homes of his district. When he died Grisell herself did the visiting. Of course, it was the way they carried out these activities that mattered most. The fact was they were welcome when they called, welcome not just for the little gifts they often brought, but welcome for themselves.

In December 1888 Grisell made history. On that day she was set apart as the first deaconess of the Church of Scotland. The service — which she called her 'wedding day' — was conducted in her own church by her old minister, Dr Allardyce. The idea of reviving the office of deaconess had come from Professor Charteris and his energetic Christian Life and Work Committee who also started the *Life and Work* magazine and launched the Woman's Guild. They had seen the Protestant Churches in Europe achieve great things with women workers and felt that there was both the need and the opportunity in Scotland. Grisell was the first to volunteer.

Grisell was an eloquent speaker and she took the chair at the first conference of the Woman's Guild, a memorable occasion for all present. Grisell was the first president of the Guild. It was important that these new ventures — which were not without their critics — should be given a good start, important that the deaconesses and the Guild were seen to be fulfilling a real purpose. Grisell met that need.

Only weeks after the Edinburgh conference Grisell fell ill. Her condition quickly worsened. On Christmas Eve they took her back to Mellerstain to be buried beside the family she had loved and honoured so well.

The new Deaconess Hospital in Edinburgh was named after her. Memorials were erected in Bowden and Newtown St Boswells. She had, after all, made history. But she and her brother Robert were best remembered for the love and the kindness they had brought to the humblest homes and the poorest people.

Mary Slessor
(1848–1915)

Psalm 3:6
> I am not afraid of ten thousands of people
> who have set themselves against me round about.

Mary had her own comment on this verse. She wrote it down on the margin of her Bible: 'God and one are always a majority.' Those seven words tell us a lot about the red-headed mill girl who became the White Queen of Okoyong.

Mary had always been interested in foreign mission. As a child she had listened enthralled as her mother read from *The Missionary Record* the exciting stories from China, India and — most exciting of all — the stories of the new work begun in tropical West Africa, in a place called Calabar. Her older brother Robert said he would be a missionary when he grew up and the children played at missionaries and natives.

Not that there was any likelihood that Robert Slessor would ever be a missionary. He was needed at home. There were seven children to be fed and clothed and the big ones had to earn a wage as soon as possible. Mary herself was 11 when she started as a 'half-timer' in Baxters' Mill.

Poverty was never far from their door. The Slessor family had moved to Dundee from Aberdeen in search of work. Both parents worked, the mother in the mill and the father as a shoemaker. He, however, was by now fighting a losing battle against alcohol and ill health. Illness hung like a cloud over the family. Four Slessor children died, including Robert the would-be missionary.

Mary Slessor was trapped, like so many others, by circumstances. Her life seemed to be firmly set. What could she do but go on drudging at the loom? The family needed the money and there was no other job available. That seemed to be that.

If, as a young Christian with strong convictions, she felt she had to do something to spread the Gospel, well, could she not collect funds? And if she had to *do* something herself, could she

27

not be a missionary here in Dundee? Were there not dark corners enough at home without going away to any dark continent? So Mary became a worker with the Queen Street Mission. Before long she had encountered her first savages and shown the courage that was to characterise her whole life.

Yet Mary Slessor still was not content. She felt that she had to go. For 16 years she had toiled in the mills, for 16 years she had kept the family together. She would go on supporting them. But now Calabar was calling for more workers, for women workers, calling for her, Mary Slessor. Had they not just heard that David Livingstone had died, died to open up the way for others? Others had to follow where he had led. Mary had to go.

In May 1875 Mary Slessor applied for service. In December she learned that she had been accepted. The following August she sailed, heading for Calabar and the white man's grave.

The story of Mary Slessor in Africa has often been told. At first she stayed in Duke Town on the coast with the Andersons. A great-hearted couple, they soon taught her what missionary work in Calabar meant. Then she moved on. The folk at home needed money and, to meet their need, Mary asked for a station of her own. This would give her enough money to keep herself alive and send home. She was sent to Old Town. This was arguably the most backward and difficult station.

Mary's time in the station was taken up with school work, with training her girls, with service to the sick, and with rescuing twins. It was the local custom to kill twins at birth. This was one of the 'old fashions' that missionaries fought hard to change. Other traditions, trial by the poisonous esere bean and human sacrifice, were also to cause Mary problems. Good work was done in Old Town. Yet Mary still was restless. There were tribes upriver to be reached. Again, she had to go.

In August 1888 she set out by canoe. She had got her wish: she was going to work among the lawless people of Okoyong. There she set to work with her usual vigour and gradually won the confidence of the people, turning them to trade and away from drinking and fighting. Her influence with the tribe was so great that she was appointed vice-consul. She was really the only white person who could control them. Recognising her love for them, they valued her wisdom and were happy to bring their disputes before her.

The old restlessness had not died out. At Okoyong she saw

something of the slave-dealing Aro tribe. She moved to the town of Itu. Soon afterwards a church was built and a small hut. She wanted it to be recognised as a proper station, a base for further outreach. That it was a natural centre was shown, she argued, by the fact that it was the slave-mart. Itu got its station and a medical centre. Mary moved on.

This was the pattern of her work in Calabar. She was a pioneer and more. She inspired her colleagues and she won the affection of the native tribes. Not surprisingly the years took their toll. She grew weaker and was sometimes very ill. Yet she soldiered on, saying only, 'If I have done anything it has been quite easy, for the Master went before.' On she went, journeying through her huge district, going where others would not go, until the journey came to an end just before dawn on a January morning in 1915.

The odds against Mary Slessor even setting out for Calabar had been enormous. The odds against her being able to do so much good were incalculable. But to Mary there was nothing so very strange about it. After all, God had been with her, and 'God and one are always a majority.'

John Howard
(1726–1790)

[1] Hear a just cause, O LORD;
    attend to my cry!
    Give ear to my prayer from lips free
    of deceit!
[2] From thee let my vindication come!
    Let thy eyes see the right!

[3] If thou triest my heart, if thou visitest
    me by night,
    if thou testest me, thou wilt find
    no wickedness in me;
    my mouth does not transgress.
[4] With regard to the works of men,
    by the word of thy lips
    I have avoided the ways of the
    violent.
[5] My steps have held fast to thy paths,
    my feet have not slipped.

[6] I call upon thee, for thou wilt answer
    me, O God;
    incline thy ear to me, hear my
    words.
[7] Wondrously show thy steadfast love,
    O saviour of those who seek refuge
    from their adversaries at thy right
    hand.

[8] Keep me as the apple of the eye;
    hide me in the shadow of thy
    wings,
[9] from the wicked who despoil me,
    my deadly enemies who surround
    me.

[10] They close their hearts to pity;
    with their mouths they speak ar-
    rogantly.

[11] They track me down; now they sur-
round me;
> they set their eyes to cast me to the
> ground.

[12] They are like a lion eager to tear,
> as a young lion lurking in ambush.

[13] Arise, O LORD! confront them, overthrow them!
> Deliver my life from the wicked by
> thy sword,

[14] from men by thy hand, O LORD,
> from men whose portion in life is
> of the world.

> May their belly be filled with what
> thou hast stored up for them;
> may their children have more than
> enough;
> may they leave something over to
> their babes.

[15] As for me, I shall behold thy face in
righteousness;
> when I awake, I shall be satisfied
> with beholding thy form.

Among those boarding the *Hanover* that day was a young widower from Hackney. His name was John Howard, and he was going for a holiday. His merchant father had left him an ample fortune and he liked best to spend his time and his money in travel. He was going to visit Lisbon to see for himself the results of the great earthquake there.

Some of his friends thought the visit rather dangerous. It was to be more dangerous than they imagined. Out at sea the *Hanover* was intercepted by a French privateer and Howard found himself not in Lisbon but in Brest, not as a tourist but as a prisoner. Conditions in that prison were ghastly. And Howard, although regaining his freedom before long, never forgot his experience. In fact it changed his whole life.

He settled in the Bedfordshire village of Cardington. And there he began the philanthropic work that was to make him famous. However, it was his appointment in 1773 as high-sheriff for the county that really gave him the opportunity to make a very personal contribution to reform. Part of his duty as high-sheriff was to inspect the local prisons. There he discovered that bad conditions were not confined to France. He was so upset by the treatment suffered not only by criminals but by debtors and even by untried prisoners that he decided to do something. So began his tour of jails in England, Scotland and Ireland.

Howard was taking a considerable risk in carrying out these visits. Cells were universally damp and unwholesome, ill-lit and badly ventilated, a perfect breeding ground for disease. He was well aware of the danger. He said, 'Trusting in Divine Providence and believing myself in the way of my duty I visit the most noxious cells and while doing so I fear no evil.'

He treasured the text above during these visits, a text that seemed to speak to his situation. It was the fifth verse of the 17th Psalm — 'My steps have held fast to thy paths'. This, he felt sure, was the road he was meant to travel, this was the work he was meant to do, and so he undertook it with the prayer from that Psalm that God would indeed hold him up.

Howard was a deeply religious man and his notebooks record his experiences and his reaction to them. He often expressed himself in the language of the Psalms, and this particular Psalm seems to have had a special place in his affections.

In 1774 he reported on his visits to the House of Commons. Two acts were soon passed in response to his findings. One enforced higher standards of cleanliness. The other abolished the old system of jailers' fees, a system that had led to all sorts of abuse. In themselves these changes were important. Howard, however, far from satisfied, felt he had only just begun.

Once more he set out on his investigations. He extended his travel to the continent. In May 1783 while visiting at Lille he came down with jail fever. For some time he was seriously ill but he recovered, expressing his gratitude in the words of his beloved Psalms. Four years later he published the results of these visits, stating fully and clearly the conditions he had uncovered. Again people listened. And again, as the result of his agitation, things were done. Some new prisons were built and other reforms carried through. Still Howard was not satisfied.

From 1785 he devoted his attention to hospitals. He was concerned chiefly with arresting the spread of disease. Once more he turned to Europe to gather facts. Years of investigation produced his *Account of the Principal Lazarettos of Europe*. For this book he chose a text for the title page, inspired again by the Psalms, 'O let the sighing of the prisoners come before Thee' (Ps 79:11).

In 1789 he set off on another journey. This time he was determined to pursue his investigations in the Russian military hospitals. He was at Kherson by the Dneiper River when he fell ill. Within days he was dead, a victim of typhus fever.

Howard had always known this might be his fate. Before he left for Russia he chose the inscription for his memorial, left instructions for his funeral, and selected the text for the funeral sermon. It came from Psalm 17, the Psalm that had meant so much to him, and from the last verse: 'as for me, I shall behold thy face in righteousness; when I awake, I shall be satisfied with beholding thy form.'

'That text,' he wrote, 'is the most appropriate to my feelings of any that I know . . . I can indeed join with the Psalmist.'

The great orator Edmund Burke paid tribute to Howard. Speaking of his travels as 'a voyage of discovery, a circumnavigation of charity', he emphasised all that Howard had done and suffered for others. It was a noble statement. But more precious to John Howard than the sincere compliments of his countrymen were the words of the psalmist, which had often brought him comfort and strength and which so aptly sum up his life and work.

B

Margaret Wilson
(*c*1667–1685)

Psalm 25:7

> Remember not the sins of my youth,
> or my transgressions;
> according to thy steadfast love remember me,
> for thy goodness' sake, O Lord!

There are those who say that it never happened. Other things, yes, but not this. It was a cruel age and dark deeds were done. But this cannot be true. That two women should be drowned, tied to the stake and drowned, and that for a matter of words; no, even then during the worst of the persecution, even in 1685, forever remembered as the killing year, it cannot be true.

Yet it did happen. The evidence is quite clear. The ground has been thoroughly covered by historians and the fact is beyond doubt. On 11 May 1685 Margaret McLauchlan and Margaret Wilson were drowned. They were taken from the jail and were tied to stakes set in the channel of the Bladnoch Water where it runs to meet the Solway tide, and there they were executed by drowning. It was a legal execution. The Privy Council had decreed that while men who refused to disown the Covenanters were to be hanged, women were to be drowned. That was the law.

Originally there had been three prisoners in Wigtown jail. There was Margaret McLauchlan, an old widow from Kirkinner Parish, and the two Wilson girls, the teenage daughters of Gilbert Wilson, farmer in Glenvernock. Brought to trial for their Covenanting sympathies, they each refused the Abjuration Oath, the standard test of the time. To them this refusal meant honouring Christ Jesus as the only head of the Church. To the government it meant treason against the king. All three were sentenced to death.

Gilbert Wilson was frantic. He himself had always been very careful to keep on the right side of the law and although his children had already reduced him to poverty with their precious

Covenants, he would do anything to save them. He scraped together the hundred pounds needed to secure the release of his younger daughter, a girl of 13. But Margaret he could not save.

On the 11 May the two women were brought out through the town. Major Winram had his soldiers mount guard. There would be no rescues that day. They took one of the stakes and set it further out. There they tied old Margaret McLauchlan. Margaret Wilson they tied to a stake nearer the town where she could see the water coming in and watch as her companion drowned.

Of course, they were hoping it would all be too much for her. They wanted her to break down and recant. The old woman might be stubborn, but a young girl surely could not face such a death, not when a few simple words could save her. She only had to accept the oath, that was all, a 'yes' for a 'no' and she would be free.

As the Solway ran in they heard her singing. The words came clear and sweet. Margaret Wilson was singing Psalm 25:7.

She had her Bible and she read from Romans 8. Then she prayed. By now the water was rising fast. Just as her head went under an order was given and soldiers plunged in and pulled her out. She was taken to dry ground and the question was put to her: would she not pray for King Charles? Would she not say 'God save the king?'

'Yes,' she gasped. 'Yes. God save the king if he will. It is his salvation I desire.' Friends and family among the crowd clamoured for her release. 'She has said it,' they cried. 'She has said it.'

Major Winram stepped forward. This was his moment, the moment he had planned for so cleverly, the moment when the rebel would break down and give in. He asked her quietly, 'Will you take the oath?'

And Margaret Wilson said, 'No.' With freedom to be had for a word she said, 'I will not. I am one of Christ's children. Let me go.' There was no more talk. They took her back and thrust her into the water. Tradition records that the town officer used his halbert to push her head under, saying 'Tak' anither drink, hinny.'

Some have tried to claim that there was a reprieve issued in Edinburgh ten days earlier. If there was, it never reached Wigtown. Margaret McLauchlan and Margaret Wilson were most certainly drowned. And they died bravely for the cause they loved.

Two other Covenanter women, Isabel Alison and Marion Harvie, had gone to the scaffold in Edinburgh singing Psalm 23. Margaret Wilson found her courage in the cold waters of the Bladnoch from Psalm 25.

> Oh guard my life, and deliver me;
> let me not be put to shame, for I take refuge in thee.

Thomas Hately
(1815–1867)

Psalm 43:3

> O send thy light forth and thy truth;
> let them be guides to me,
> And bring me to thine holy hill,
> ev'n where thy dwellings be.

The original painting hangs in the Free Church Presbytery Hall in Edinburgh. It took the artist, David Octavius Hill, some 20 years to paint. It represents the scene in May 1843 when the Deed of Demission was signed by those ministers who left the National Church to form the Free Church.

It took Hill all those years to complete because he wished to show all those who were involved in the event, together with others who were not in fact present that day but who had lent their support to the cause. To capture the likenesses of nearly 500 men, Hill — who was a pioneer of photography — went after them with his camera, and then gave them their place in the picture. It is interesting to see that the minister who is shown signing the deed is Dr Patrick Macfarlan of Greenock, chosen because he signed away the richest living.

In the forefront of the painting are men such as Hugh Miller, the famous Cromarty geologist, who had played his part in the struggle as editor of *The Witness*. Also depicted prominently is a dark-haired man in his late 20s, sitting in solemn thought: Thomas Hately.

Thomas Hately was born at Greenlaw in Berwickshire and later worked in Edinburgh as a printer. As a lad he had carried proofs to Sir Walter Scott in Castle Street. On one visit he was kept waiting so long, he fell asleep! Eventually he became a manager at Constable's, an Edinburgh printing firm. But the great passion of his life was music.

With encouragement from Robert Smith, a Paisley weaver who had become precentor at St George's and was widely respected as a composer, young Hately began his career in Church music at Leith. From there he came to serve as precentor at St Mary's Parish Church, at the time regarded as one of the great 'prizes' of the city.

And Hately walked out of the General Assembly in May 1843. Much as he loved his work, well as it rewarded him, he walked out. For he, too, was convinced of the rightness of the Free Church case and he decided to take his stand with the ministers and elders who walked out of the '43 Assembly.

He went on to make a great contribution to the development of Church music. Recognising his unique talent, the Free Church leaders not only made him the Assembly precentor, they sent him out to travel the country, training teachers and conducting classes. Hately made this his full-time work. Certainly it kept him busy. It so happened that there was widespread demand throughout the country for better singing. Most congregations had a sadly limited repertoire of tunes: 'the Psalms of David to the tunes of David' as Dr Guthrie's old servant would say. And, it seemed, there were only a dozen tunes in that canon. Thomas Hately proved to be the man for the hour.

His classes were very popular. At Greenock it is said 900 attended the class, while others were almost as large. Hately began to collect suitable tunes for his eager pupils. Some were old tunes — like those in his 'Gaelic Psalm Tunes' — which he gathered and wrote down. Others he wrote himself. Hately composed some 40 tunes for the Psalms. For years melodies such as 'Knox', 'Zwingli', 'Glencairn' and 'Huntingtower' were very popular, and a few, such as 'Leuchars' and 'Nenthorn' have survived to the present.

Through his work as a composer, as an editor, and as a teacher, Thomas Hately did much. He enabled his countrymen to sing more Psalms to a richer variety of tunes. Unlike some, he was prepared to see the introduction of hymns in worship and, in particular, the tune 'Nenthorn' was written specifically for the hymn 'Nearer my God to Thee'. It was written not for his own Church but for the Church of Scotland and their *Hymn Tune Book* of 1865. Nonetheless, the Psalms were very special to him. And one Psalm had very precious associations.

Back in 1843, on that May morning when the first Assembly of the Free Church gathered in Tanfield Hall, the building was darkened by heavy thunder clouds. The mood was sombre. But when the Moderator, Dr Chalmers, gave out the Psalm and Thomas Hately rose to lead the singing, as the first line was raised — 'O send thy light forth and thy truth' — the cloud lifted, and the sun broke through. It was a wonderful moment and no one who was there would ever forget that Psalm with its prayer for light, and the way that prayer seemed to be answered.

The Psalms have had a particularly rich influence on Scottish worship and on the personal devotion of many generations of Scottish people. This has been due in no small measure to the contribution of Thomas Hately who gave the music to match the words and who, in his own way, helped the light to shine for others.

Esther Beecher
(1800–1878)

Psalm 111:2

> Great are the works of the Lord,
> studied by all who have pleasure in them.

P G Wodehouse reminds us that 'aunts aren't gentlemen'. Even the good aunts, the Aunt Dahlias, can cause problems. However, Bertie Wooster at his silliest would still have recognised Aunt Esther as one of the right sort. Aunt Esther, Esther Beecher to give her hcr full name, was just the kind of aunt that every family should have. That was certainly the verdict of her nephews and nieces.

The great thing about Aunt Esther was that she was never stuck for a story. There you were, lying in bed, feeling sick and rather sorry for yourself, when the door would open and in would come Aunt Esther. Right away the room seemed brighter. Perhaps it was the way she smiled. Maybe it was the way those brown eyes sparkled. But down she would sit and start to talk. And she would be so cheerful and so interesting that pretty soon you would forget to feel ill.

She never failed. She always had something new to tell and it was always something you wanted to hear. Like the little nephew who later confided to his sister, 'Only think! Aunt Esther has told me 19 rat stories all in a string!'

Aunt Esther was interested in natural history. She seemed to know about every plant that grew and every animal that lived. But then she seemed to know about everything. There is no doubt that she was an exceptionally well-read lady, who could talk to professors about chemistry and argue over philosophy. Of course, they were a clever lot, these Beechers. Her brother Lyman was said to be one of the best preachers in the land, even before he went off to Ohio to become a college president.

But the thing about Aunt Esther was not that she knew so much. Other people were clever too. No, the thing about Aunt

Esther was just this: she was interested. In everything! That was it. She made you want to find out about everything. And she made you want to share your discoveries. Just like she did.

Aunt Esther was a great influence on the family, especially on her brother's children. There were thirteen of them and all seven boys were to follow their father and become preachers. The most famous was Henry Ward Beecher. However, it was one of the girls, Harriet, who became best known. This she did by telling a story about things she had found out. She had gone with her husband, Professor Calvin Stowe, on a fact-finding visit to Kentucky. There she had learned something about life among the Negro slaves. And as a consequence she wrote *Uncle Tom's Cabin*.

It is questionable if any novel ever had a greater effect on society. Students of literature will argue that her later books are better written and less patronising. They may be right. However, nothing can alter the fact that *Uncle Tom's Cabin* struck home in a way that few books ever have.

Perhaps the slaves would have been freed anyway. Perhaps there were other issues dividing the American states and leading to the vast horrors of the Civil War. But Harriet Beecher Stowe wrote one of the most important books ever.

Would it have been written if there had been no Aunt Esther? It was Aunt Esther who, by her happy example, encouraged the children to look at the world around them and to talk about what they saw. And there was something more. The Beechers were a genuinely devout family, and Aunt Esther had another reason for her enthusiastic pursuit of knowledge.

As the children got older they began to wonder just how their favourite aunt knew so much. Perhaps they had even heard some whispers that it wasn't quite right for a lady to know so much. Anyway the day came when some of the older children asked her outright. How did she know so much about so many things? Why did she think it so important?

Aunt Esther told them. She took them to the place of final authority: the Bible, and she pointed out Psalm 111:2. There was Aunt Esther's inspiration, there the secret of her glad finding out. There, too, was the challenge for the children, to seek out the works of the Lord — and to tell what they found.

George Matheson
(1842–1906)

Psalm 116:15

> Precious in the sight of the Lord
> is the death of his saints.

Years later Dr Somerville told the story of George Matheson's first sermon. The first sermon is obviously a special event in the life of every minister but in those days, back in the 1860s, there was a particular tradition to be observed by aspiring preachers. During their first term at the Divinity Hall, students would prepare a sermon on a text given by the professor. Once that sermon had been heard and commented on by the professor, and by fellow-students, the thing was to secure an early opportunity to deliver it in a church. It was also very much part of the custom to have the other students come in strength to that service. Whether their presence would be a help or a hindrance to the preacher is open to question.

In due course George Matheson passed on the word to his colleagues. He would be preaching the next Sunday evening, taking a service in the parish schoolroom of the College Church in the High Street. Matheson was an outstanding student and his friends were eager to be there.

The first surprise came when he gave out his text, Psalm 116:15. This was not the text of his classroom sermon. This was altogether different. So was the sermon. Matheson had prepared specially for this service. He had something he wanted to say.

Dr Somerville was a young student then. He was to hear — and himself to preach — many sermons. This one he never forgot. It had, he later said, 'the freshness and originality' that were to distinguish Matheson's work. In that sermon, his first sermon, he spoke of death. Death, he argued, was but 'the gate to higher work and purer joys'. To Somerville and his friends it was an amazing performance; they came away deep in thought, impressed by the man and moved by the message.

It was not chance that had led George Matheson to this theme. This was to him a great and wonderful truth. To the end of his ministry it was to be a constant note in his preaching and writing: this life is but the beginning, fulness comes only hereafter.

He was a Glasgow boy, born the second of eight children in the south side of the city, before the family in their growing prosperity moved west. His father was a successful businessman. George was just 18 months old when they discovered that there was something wrong with his eyes. Specialists were called in. They could do nothing. Gradually through his childhood years his sight failed. By the age of 18 he was blind.

This tremendous handicap might have ruined his life. George was highly intelligent and he had once had hopes of pursuing an academic life. Now, on the very threshold, the door had closed in his face. It was a bitter thing to be 18 and blind. It could have been a fatal blow, but George overcame his hurt.

He did go to university and, despite his blindness, went on to gain great distinction. As a minister he continued his studies. In all this he was helped by his sister. With a patience no less than his own she did his writing and his reading. She became his closest companion and best friend. When he became a minister she stayed with him, taking on new duties, and she remained with him to the end.

Matheson's name is always associated with the village of Innellan. He went there in 1868 after a period as assistant at his home church, Sandyford in Glasgow. When he arrived the church was but a chapel of ease under the parish church at Dunoon. Soon, however, his great gifts as a preacher and writer began to draw the crowds. Within two years the chapel gained full status. Summer visitors came to Innellan just to hear Matheson. One man, we know, came for 13 years and when Matheson left he never returned. He was also an earnest pastor and his cheerful face with its neat beard was known and loved throughout the Cowal peninsula.

It was here that Matheson became known as a writer. He produced some weighty volumes of theology as well as lighter, more meditative, pieces that were widely popular. More significantly, it was here that he wrote his most famous hymn, the beautiful 'O Love that wilt not let me go'.

Matheson was called to Edinburgh to St Bernard's Church. The congregation had come through a difficult time but here, it was felt, was the man for the hour. So it proved. For 13 years he exercised a happy ministry. All sorts of people came to sit under him but it was perhaps the young people, especially the students, who got the greatest 'lift' from his message.

When this brave and gifted man finished his course it was remarked that 'It was not night but light that had fallen on him.' It was exactly the way he had always felt himself about death. This was the same hope he had given to others ever since that first sermon in the High Street.

Alexander Murray
(1775–1813)

Psalm 118:19

> O set ye open unto me
> the gates of righteousness;
> Then I will enter into them,
> And I the Lord will bless.

A popular 'run' for people in the south-west of Scotland is a visit to Murray's Monument at Talnotry. It stands on a hill just to the north of the A712 some seven miles from Newton Stewart and about eleven miles from New Galloway. There is a good, if somewhat steep, path from the car park to the 70-foot granite obelisk that bears the name of Alexander Murray DD. The inscription tells us that Murray, 'a Shepherd Boy on these Hillsides', came from a humble home at Dunkitterick to serve as minister of Urr and as Professor of Oriental Languages at Edinburgh University.

The truly poignant part of the story is conveyed by the dates: Murray was born in October 1775, he died in April 1813. He served as professor for a few months only.

Dunkitterick was a small cottage set in a wild glen shut in by high hills, where Robert Murray brought his wife in January 1775. She was his second wife, the first having died some five years earlier. In October Alexander was born. The father was a shepherd, like his father before him, and the four sons of the first marriage had all followed in the family tradition. It was assumed, not unreasonably, that Alexander too would become a shepherd.

Alexander Murray might well have become a shepherd and, in fact, he spent two years on the hill. However, it became clear during those two years that something was not quite right. The boy — he was just 12 — seemed unable to account for his flock. Sheep were always wandering. Was he lazy, or careless, his father wondered. The other lads had not had these problems. He went out himself with Alexander and was astonished to see the boy count a rock as a sheep. Only then did he realise that Alexander had poor eyesight. Some other work would have to be found. (With these eyes Alexander would never be a shepherd.)

The father knew the lad was clever. He had taught Alexander to read and write before sending him for some months to the school in New Galloway. With no more education than that he had already worked as a tutor to two families. Might it not be worth while sending him back to school now? Alexander therefore returned to his studies. His hope was to become a merchant's clerk and work in the West Indies or America. The warmer climate would be good for him, they all said, for he was often ill.

Alexander loved to study. He discovered that he had a particular aptitude for languages. At Minnigaf School he mastered Latin and French and was introduced to Greek. The schoolmaster was an alcoholic, but he could still recognise and encourage such a rare talent. By the age of 16 Alexander had learned Hebrew. He then took up Anglo-Saxon, Welsh and Arabic. For diversion he wrote poetry.

James McHarg, a family friend, was a tea smuggler. His trade took him often to Edinburgh, from where he would bring back books for the scholar. He wanted to assist the young man and tried to get his translations and poems taken by a publisher. He failed in this scheme but from his contacts in academic circles he learned that a lad like Alexander had a fair chance of winning a place at university. Then he could really show his paces.

So Alexander Murray went to university. By 1802 he had completed courses in philosophy and theology and was licensed as a preacher. After some time as a literary editor, he was presented to the parish of Urr in Kirkcudbrightshire, where he married a local girl and settled down to a busy and happy life.

In 1811 there occurred the incident that made him famous and changed his life. A dispatch from Abyssinia arrived at the court of King George III. There were already sufficient problems at court without seeking any more complications and it was therefore agreed that a tactful reply would have to be sent. That, however, was going to be rather difficult. No one could translate the message! Then a former envoy, Henry Salt, remembered having come across some of Murray's writings. Perhaps this was the man to rescue the court. An approach was made, Murray was able to effect a translation, the correct reply was sent, and everyone was happy.

The following year Murray was persuaded to apply for the Professorship of Oriental Languages at Edinburgh University. There was stiff competition for the post but he was elected. In a way, nothing worse could have happened. Determined to fulfil his duties honourably he drove himself too hard and his frail strength gave way. By the following March he was confined to his room. He got worse. Although he now knew he would never deliver the lectures he had been preparing, he continued to work in his room.

By the middle of April it was obvious that the end was near. His wife was by his side. On the night of the 14th he could not sleep. He lay awake and his wife heard him repeating Psalm 118:19. She joined with him, repeating the next lines:

> This is the gate of God, by it
>   the just shall enter in.
> Thee will I praise, for thou me heard'st
>   and hast my safety been.

And it was thus, with this quiet assurance, that the door did open and the young professor finished his journey in peace.

Robert Napier
(1791–1876)

Proverbs 22:29

> Do you see a man skilful in his work?
> he will stand before Kings;
> he will not stand before obscure
> men.

It is, we like to believe, a Scottish tradition that the local lad who makes good is not allowed to become conceited. 'Him? I kent his faither,' about sums it up. All the more remarkable, then, that tribute paid to Robert Napier by one who knew him and his family. Old Donald Macleod wrote that Napier reminded him of a verse from the Book of Proverbs, the verse that runs, 'Do you see a man skilful in his work? he will stand before kings' (Prov 22:29).

Robert Napier was diligent in his business and his business flourished. And if he did not meet many kings he did once kiss a royal princess . . .

Napier was born in Dumbarton where his father was well known as a blacksmith and millwright. A bright lad at school, Robert learned his trade with his father and then set off to make his fortune. His first attempts to find work in Edinburgh were less than successful but he did serve for a time with the lighthouse engineer Robert Stevenson.

It was in 1815 that he started his own business in Glasgow, in the Greyfriars Wynd. Then he moved to the Camlachie Foundry owned by his cousin David. There he built his first engine. Two years later he built his first successful marine engine, for the paddle steamer *Leven* which ran between Dumbarton and Glasgow. The engine is now on display in the shopping precinct at Dumbarton.

Moving to new premises, he went on to develop a great reputation, which could not but be enhanced when two steam yachts fitted with his engines won first and second place in a prestigious race. People began to take heed of young Mr Napier. In 1835 he built his first ocean-going engines and in 1840 he began what was to prove a long and happy relationship with the British and North American Royal Mail Company, later known as the Cunard Company.

The next year he embarked on a new venture. He established an iron shipyard at Govan with another Dumbarton man, William Denny, as his chief draughtsman. When the yard launched the paddle steamer *Persia* a couple of years later the public was astounded at the size of the vessel. Bigger ships were to follow as the yard won orders from the navy.

And where did all this leave Napier the man? It left him in considerable comfort at his home at West Shandon. Handing over the running of his business to his sons, Robert built up a great collection of paintings, together with a considerable amount of fascinating curios. His home drew many visitors from all parts. And so he came to kiss a princess.

The fact was Robert Napier, now in his 70s, had decided to welcome all lady visitors with what he called 'a Shandon salute'. That is, he kissed them on the cheek. So when the Princess Louise arrived with her husband, the Marquis, old Robert promptly kissed her. He got away with it too.

Nor did he forget his old town. Every New Year he would send the Kirk Session a donation. They were to see that it went to help those in need. And there was no need to tell everyone where it came from.

When he died in 1876 he was brought back to Dumbarton. A special train brought 1400 of his workmen to follow his coffin to the parish church. The local shops and businesses closed and the ships in the harbour and in the yards flew their flags at half-mast.

Of course, he was an important man. It was but right that the town would mark his funeral. It need not mean that he was a good man, nor a man greatly loved. But the evidence is there that Robert Napier had won both the respect and affection of many. He had made a significant contribution to Clyde shipbuilding, proving that steam engines could be made to drive the biggest ships. He had shown what hard work and enterprise could achieve. And he had not forgotten where he came from.

Richmal Crompton
(1890–1969)

Proverbs 29:23

> A man's pride will bring him low,
> but he who is lowly in spirit will
> obtain honour.

Richmal always insisted it was her brother Jack. He, she said, was the original William of her stories. People did wonder. After all, Richmal Crompton Lamburn — to give her her full name — had never married and had no boys of her own. On top of which she had gone to a girls' school (for daughters of the clergy!) and she had spent her early adult life teaching Latin and Greek to girls. How, then, it was asked, could she write so well about boys?

Young brother Jack was the obvious answer, except for one thing. He himself denied the connection. He went further. He said that Richmal had based her character on that of another writer. He could not remember the name of this other writer but he persisted in his story.

From time to time people have tried to identify this mysterious writer and his boy. Some have pointed, rather unconvincingly, to Eden Philpotts and his *The Human Boy*. Others have argued for the American Booth Tarkington and his Penrod stories. There are many superficial similarities — as indeed there would be with stories about boys of the same age and robust nature — but the differences are obvious. And there is Robert Green.

Robert Green is the boy in a short story called 'One Crowded Hour' which Richmal wrote for a women's magazine. He is younger than William but his character is unmistakably the same. Here then is Richmal trying something new; she was already writing romantic stories with some success. Her own explanation still seems the most satisfactory; she did recall incidents from her brother's childhood — she later drew inspiration from a nephew — and, as she said, 'Once you've thought of a boy the rest is easy.'

So why should her brother deny it and suggest that his sister had 'lifted' her boy from another book? It must be said that when that accusation was made the two were not on the best of terms. And, anyway, was it really so very flattering to be thought of as the original William? There was, too, the fact that William's father was apt to remark in despair, 'The boy is mad.' Jack's relationship with his father had been too difficult for him to enjoy any such allusion.

Does it matter? It certainly would have mattered to Richmal. The reputation of her books mattered greatly to her. The financial rewards they brought meant little, a trait she had inherited from her father the minister. Although she enjoyed spending money on her family and friends, and also gave freely to many charities, she had a genuine unconcern for material things.

Nor did she revel in her well-earned fame. She hated being the centre of attraction and avoided public engagements as much as possible. It is said that many of her old acquaintances from school and college never learned that the little Miss Lamburn they remembered was the celebrated writer. She had no desire to be a celebrity.

Her attitude to life is summed up best in a verse that she wrote in a black book that she carried with her. That verse, which she underlined carefully, was the guiding principle of her working life. Richmal's faith was very real. She could face the ill health and disabilities of her declining years with quiet cheerfulness, 'simply trusting God', and getting on with her writing. She was working on the 38th William book at the end.

Richmal might have remained a teacher who wrote had it not been for an attack of polio. Although she made a good recovery she was unable to go back to school work. So instead she became a writer — who taught. Richmal Crompton does teach us. Through her books and by her life she makes us stop and think about the things that really matter.

Lewis Carroll
(1832–1898)

Ecclesiastes 9:10

Whatever your hand finds to do, do it with your might; for there is no work or thought or knowledge or wisdom in Sheol, to which you are going.

Lewis Carroll we all know. *Alice's Adventures in Wonderland* and *Through the Looking Glass* still hold their special place, enjoyed by children and adults alike. Perhaps we know some of his other writings. And, almost certainly, we remember hearing something about the man himself.

To begin with, we recall that Lewis Carroll was not his real name. He was Charles Lutwidge Dodgson. We know, too, that Charles Lutwidge Dodgson was shy, painfully shy, and felt most at home when among children, especially among young girls. Which is how *Alice* came to be written. Again, we might well remember that he was a clergyman who spent his working life at university teaching mathematics. And perhaps we have heard that he had a delight in photography.

All of which, while true, might give us the wrong picture of the man. There was another side to the gentle and retiring don. Certainly he was no idler, dreaming his life away in an ivory tower. On the contrary.

While a small boy at Richmond School, before he went to Rugby, Charles Dodgson earned a surprising reputation. As a fighter! Having suffered from bullying as a new boy, he set himself up as the champion of the little fellows and revealed a rare skill as a boxer. So much so that his name was held in high regard long after he left. All his life, he retained this willingness to take up the cause of the weak and the suffering. He was notably generous and, in his own way, truly brave.

He was also a good walker, and thought nothing of doing 18 miles in an afternoon. He once did 29 without feeling tired. And that's not counting the distances he covered on his tricycle!

Dodgson was a hard worker, and a very systematic one. He always got up at the same time and, when in residence, always attended the college service. He took his afternoon walk, either alone or sometimes with a child — in which case he didn't go so far but talked the whole time. Then in the evening he settled down to work. His preparation for his class work, which he took with the utmost seriousness, his writing, and his other studies would sometimes keep him out of bed until the early hours of the morning. He was also a painstaking correspondent, keeping a record of all his letters and devising his own system of cross-reference. This was doubtless an invaluable tool for it records some 98 721 letters.

Stuart Dodgson Collingwood, Lewis Carroll's nephew and biographer tells us that Carroll had a rule of life which comes from Ecclesiastes 9:10. That text was his motto, and he made it his business to live it out. As he grew older he also found uplift in that text from John 9:4: 'night comes when no one can work.' To the last he thought nothing of a six-hour stint at his desk.

That Dodgson, as a clergyman, should find inspiration from the Bible is not at all surprising. However, it does raise a question: if he was a clergyman why did he never seek a church, and why was he reluctant to preach? There is a simple answer. The son of a parish minister, he knew from an early age that he was not cut out to follow in his father's footsteps. But to stay on at Christ Church it was necessary to 'take orders'. So he did.

There was nothing false about his position. He knew he could never serve in a parish. He knew he was in the right place, where his particular gifts could do most good. And he was there as a convinced Christian. In one of those letters he tells a friend, 'I owe all to him who loved me, and died on the Cross of Calvary.' His attitude to his work as his service comes across in the entry in his diary: 'May God bless the new form of life that lies before me, that I may use it according to his holy will.'

As for not preaching, well, it should be remembered that Dodgson suffered from a stammer. That in itself, and the attendant fear of upsetting a service and embarrassing a congregation, did hold him back. But he did preach occasionally; and with effect. The vicar of Westham, a village church near Eastbourne, recalls how Dodgson once preached for him and tells how the congregation of agricultural labourers and their wives 'breathlessly listened to a sermon forty minutes long — and took in every word of it'. In fact he was happiest when preaching to working people and talking to children.

He did, of course, attempt to write a children's book with a Christian moral but, despite some excellent passages, his *Sylvie and Bruno* has never been popular. However, to those who knew him, his life was just such a book with just such a message, showing how we can use all our might in the Master's service and in that service find our deepest joy and satisfaction.

Margaret Ogilvy
(1820–1896)

Isaiah 40:28

Have you not known? Have you not heard?
The Lord is the everlasting God,
   the Creator of the ends of the earth.
He does not faint or grow weary,
   his understanding is unsearchable.

She knew something was wrong. He should have been working, but he was just sitting there, slumped over the kitchen table, and looking so very miserable. What had happened? Why wasn't he writing? Writing? No, he said, he wasn't writing. He didn't think he would ever write again.

He pointed to the book open on the table, *The Master of Ballantrae* by Robert Louis Stevenson. *That* was writing. He could never hope to do anything like it. So what was the use of trying?

'Stevenson,' sniffed his mother, 'I could never thole his books.' Her son looked up, 'You have not read any of them,' he pointed out. 'And never shall,' she replied. And the spell was broken.

It became something of a game that they played, James Barrie and his mother. She did read Stevenson's book and greatly enjoyed them. There was one time she would not go to bed until she was sure that Jim Hawkins got out of the apple barrel. Yet all the time she pretended not to like Stevenson's stories. 'I would rather read your books' she would say, with Stevenson's latest under her apron.

That was Margaret Ogilvy. In this scene we see her good sense and her good humour as well as her love for her children and her pride in their achievements.

She had a delightful sense of humour and a most wonderfully happy laugh. She had laughed at first when young James came home from university to tell her he would be a writer. No, she said, he would be a minister and maybe one day a professor.

Writers, she had read, had a terrible time of it, starving in garrets and sleeping on park benches. Anyway, it was no place for decent folk, that London.

She laughed too when his articles began to appear and she discovered that he was better paid for the pieces about their old ways up in 'Thrums' than for all his serious writing. Presently her letters began to fill with memories that her clever son could write into stories. She even wondered if it would not be a wise thing to send on some of her shortbread to keep the editor sweet? Altogether Margaret Ogilvy was a great encourager.

There were many she encouraged outside the family too. She had the gift — and a very precious gift it is — of being able to help people without hurting their feelings. It was to her that other mothers ran when there was trouble. Her generosity showed itself in her attitude to the christening robe. She bought it — she wanted to be extravagant just once she said — although no one was better than herself at making clothes. All her own children were christened in it and so were hundreds of other children. Yes, hundreds. To lend that robe was one of her greatest pleasures.

She had her sorrows, Margaret Ogilvy. She lost her own mother when she was only eight. She lost two children in infancy. Then she lost her David. He was 13 when he died, this son, and he had been away at school when he fell ill. The parents were at the railway station ready to go to him, waiting to board the train, when the message came in at the telegraph office that it was already over.

In a sense she never got over it. Her health was always delicate thereafter and for months she was very weak. All the family did what they could to help her through and wee James tried hard to make her laugh again, keeping a score of every success on a piece of paper. Slowly she recovered and became once more the helper of others.

Apart from the love of her family there was another source of help in those sad months: Paraphrase 22 and the lines:

> Art thou afraid His pow'r shall fail
> When comes thy evil day?

and the answering verse:

> He gives the conquest to the weak,
> Supports the fainting heart;
> And courage in the evil hour
> His heavenly aids impart.

Based on Isaiah 40:28–31 these were her favourite lines. She had proved their promise true. When her evil day came his power had not failed. She always found comfort in these words. They were, records her son, the last thing she read, and as she read, 'I saw her timid face take courage.'

The daughter who had been her faithful nurse through the years of her old age died quite suddenly. The family were fearful how their mother would get on without her. Another evil day had come. Yet once more his power did not fail, for the ailing mother passed away the next day. The others were there by her bed — except James who was rushing home as fast as trains could bring him — and the last words they heard as Margaret Ogilvy quietly prayed were 'God' and 'love'.

Thomas Forsyth
(1822–1901)

Ezekiel 33:11

Say to them, As I live, says the Lord God, I have no pleasure in the death of the wicked, but that the wicked turn from his way and live; turn back, turn back from your evil ways; for why will you die, O house of Israel?

He should have been happy. Most folk thought he was. Indeed most people had a high opinion of Thomas Forsyth. They knew he was a decent, hard-working man who was always in employment. He came from a respectable family; had his father not been well known throughout the parish both for learning and for piety and him a fine farmer too? And here was young Thomas, a man now and married these two years. A quiet, big fellow, though famous throughout South Ayrshire for his strength: none could match him at putting the stone and few would now try him at the wrestling. Yes, of course, he must be happy.

But Thomas Forsyth was not happy. For all he was a good-living man he felt that somehow he was not right with God. Friends told him that this feeling would pass and urged him to ignore it. But the words of Ezekiel kept coming back and they gave him no rest. Forsyth knew himself to be, in God's sight, a sinner. But what to do about it?

There was a divinity student working in the parish that summer. Forsyth heard him preach and resolved to attend the Bible class called for the next Tuesday night. After coming to a few of these meetings Forsyth put himself forward as being ready for communion. The student told him he was not ready. He told him why: Forsyth was still trusting to himself and to his own goodness to win God's favour. His words came as a shock, but they were also a turning point. The student, a Mr Reid, was then able to lead Forsyth to faith.

Like many new converts, Thomas Forsyth wanted to do something right away. 'I had' he later said, 'more zeal than knowledge.

But I never saw a man yet full of zeal who remained very long in ignorance.' He began to visit the sick, and with the help of two like-minded friends, he started to hold meetings in the houses in and around Barrhill. He also taught in the local Sunday School.

Then he fell ill. This was a new and strange experience for Forsyth, who had hitherto enjoyed such robust good health. It took him five years to throw off the effects of his illness and even at that he was no longer fit for heavy manual labour. Yet, far from being despondent, Forsyth took his enforced rest as an opportunity, for he had spent only nine months at school, and began to catch up on his reading.

After some time as a cattle dealer — 'a man in this kind of business needs great grace' — he settled in the town of Maybole as a butcher. He soon found kindred spirits and attended religious meetings regularly. These meetings were supported by all the churches and all the ministers in town were involved. However, when summer came round meetings and their work stopped. Forsyth felt this was a mistake. So, with the help of John Brackenridge the country postman, he started his own meetings. Here he first began to preach. However, he felt he could do his best work as a visitor. A welcome visitor he was, too, not least because he always carried a parcel from his shop and left behind in every house something for the pot.

Six years on and things started to happen. Two evangelists were invited to town and crowds flocked to hear them. Forsyth was in the thick of it. And it was to him that many turned for guidance. People would call on him at all hours. For seven weeks he hardly got to bed as hundreds of enquirers sought him out. Nor did it end with the departure of the evangelists. The local churches all played a part in making sure that this opportunity was not lost. Great open-air meetings were held and on occasion as many as 600 would march through the town to a service, singing as they went, and drawing others with them.

Some people were not pleased. They talked of the peace being disturbed. And one night an attempt was made to arrest Forsyth at an open-air meeting. 'Who sent you?' he asked. The policeman mentioned the name of a well-known figure in the community. Forsyth nodded. 'Then go and tell him,' he said, 'that he owes me £23.12.6. If I do more damage than that I will pay the odds tomorrow.' No one tried to stop him after that. Maybe it was as well, for a number of locals were prepared to resist any attempt to interfere with their preacher.

But the stirring days did come to an end. Disagreement broke out among the workers, the movement split. Forsyth had seen the problem and had tried his hardest to prevent it. Quietly and sadly he left the meetings and went back to his visiting.

Perhaps as a result his health broke again. Therefore when he was asked to go to the village of Straiton as a missionary he was happy to go; he was tired of Maybole. He was now in his mid 50s and able for the first time to give all of his time and energy to religious work.

Forsyth stayed in Straiton for over 20 years. It is for his work there that he is best remembered. A pleasant place it was — as it still is — but this did not mean that his task was easy. The people felt that they had all the religion they needed with the weekly service in church. There was little interest in mid-week services or prayer meetings. Even his visits were at first unwelcome.

His first success came with the young people. Through them he found a door to their families. Gradually he wore down opposition and awakened interest. Nor did he confine his activities to the parish but was happy to visit the neighbouring villages. He used to say that some of his best work was done on the road, talking to those he met as he walked from place to place. He also paid two visits to Ireland.

Throughout his long and laborious life Thomas Forsyth helped many to find their Saviour. Remembering his own difficulties as a young man, and the way he was troubled by those words of Ezekiel, he never apologised for disturbing people and shaking their complacency. Many who at first were angered or amused by him lived to thank him for what he said. For himself, well, he once said, 'If two angels were sent from heaven, one to govern a nation, and the other to sweep the streets . . . the one would be as well pleased with his work as the other.' It was enough to know that even in the quiet village and the small town he had played a part for the Master. He asked no more.

William Guthrie
(1620–1665)

Hosea 13:9

> O Israel, thou has destroyed thyself;
> but in me is thine help.

Day had scarcely dawned that summer morning when the crowds began to gather. They could be seen making their way from every quarter to the church at the heart of the village. In itself, apart from the early hour, this was not unusual. For years people had come here that they might sit under the minister of Fenwick. In fact some had settled in the village just to be near William Guthrie.

Yet that day of 24 July 1664 was unusual. There was something strange about a congregation assembling here so early in the day. It showed in their faces and was there when they spoke. They had come to hear their minister for the last time. Later that morning he would be deprived of his office and, under pain of law, forbidden to preach there again. So they came, filling the church, cramming it to the doors, listening to that beloved voice. And they were ready to do whatever he asked.

These were troubled days in Scotland. Charles II had returned to the throne and the tide of persecution was sweeping over the land. Those like William Guthrie who were Covenanters, who had pledged themselves to maintain the Church of their fathers, were to conform — or be swept away. Some of them were for resistance, some were for flight, some were for surrender. Guthrie was for staying and facing the storm.

Some folk might call him a fanatic. He had, after all, always stood with the more extreme party within the Covenanting movement. Nor was this surprising for one of the great influences on his life had been his cousin James Guthrie of Stirling: in Cromwell's phrase, 'the short man who could not bow'.

Yet William Guthrie did not fit the rôle of fanatic too well. He was a laird's son, born at Pitforthie near Brechin. He was handsome and witty, a keen sportsman and a talented musician. Was that not what had first won the people to him? He had been the first minister to serve Fenwick, and the people of that moorland parish had not much enthusiasm for church services and not much use for ministers. Until, that is, William Guthrie began his work.

He would visit the outlying farms of an evening, letting the folk think he was a traveller. Once in he would charm the household with his good humour and good sense. Then — oh so casually — he would ask them how they liked their new minister. When they replied that they had never thought to go and hear the man, he would suggest they should, promising them a surprise.

Other men he met out fishing. Or on the ice in winter at curling. Or out on the moor with a gun and a well-filled bag. They came to hear him because he seemed different. They came again because he was different. Here, they discovered, was a man with a message.

A devoted pastor, a winning preacher, a man of principle, this was the one they came to hear that Sunday morning. Some 20 years he had been their minister, the only minister many of them knew, the one whose words had won their souls. What would he say?

Part of the message they had heard already. For on the previous Wednesday he had preached from Hosea. Ah, some might say, how like a Covenanter, passing by the Gospels to dwell on the Old Testament! How typical! And, to those who have never heard Guthrie nor ever seen that book of his that Dr Chalmers would later call the greatest book he ever read, to all who feel superior to a 17th-century divine preaching up the times, the choice of text might seem conclusive. For on that Wednesday Guthrie preached from Hosea 13:9. And, sure enough, he did preach at length on the sins of the Church and the nation. He did so with all his considerable power, for while he could be witty he could also be severe. He preached the truth as he saw it: a Church and people who had broken faith with God had brought down God's just anger on the nation.

But that was on the Wednesday. This is Sunday. And again Guthrie turns to Hosea, to the same passage. Only now he takes the second part of the verse for his text — But in Me is thine help. His last words will not be words of judgment but words of hope. He has warned. He now will comfort. He has been faithful, he has shown what the Church has brought on itself. Now he will point to the One who alone can forgive and heal. And for those who will face persecution in the coming days here are the everlasting arms open to hold them safe.

He will go from his church that morning, the church they built for him, and he will receive the curate who comes to depose him with great kindness. There will be no fighting. A few years on, the men of Fenwick will fight, marching out under the blue banner; they will fight and they will fall 'for Christ's Crown and Covenant'. They would have fought that day too if Guthrie had said but one word. But his wish is for peace. He has spoken out against wrong. He is prepared, if need be, to follow his cousin to the scaffold. His own health has already suffered and his days will not be long. But, if he sees the judgment coming and the storm about to break, he is not afraid.

John Brown
(1722–1787)

Micah 7:7–10

⁷ But as for me, I will look to the
LORD,
I will wait for the God of my salvation;
my God will hear me.
⁸ Rejoice not over me, O my enemy;
when I fall, I shall rise;
when I sit in darkness,
the LORD will be a light to me.
⁹ I will bear the indignation of the
LORD
because I have sinned against him,
until he pleads my cause
and executes judgment for me.
He will bring me forth to the light;
I shall behold his deliverance.
¹⁰ Then my enemy will see,
and shame will cover her who said
to me,
"Where is the LORD your God?"
My eyes will gloat over her;
now she will be trodden down
like the mire of the streets.

Which John Brown is this? This is the John Brown whose story — with one exception — is the classic tale of the Scottish lad o' pairts rising from poverty and obscurity to win an honoured place in Church and society. He is the shepherd boy who became a professor, but there is one part of his story which is strangely different.

But let's start at the beginning. John Brown was born in 1722. He was born in the tiny hamlet of Carpow, near Abernethy, a mile or so from the Tay. His father was a weaver and salmon fisher, poor enough but resolutely honest and deeply religious. When John was only 11 his father died and the mother passed away soon after. The little orphan went to work as a shepherd.

Yet thrust as he was out into the hard world, John was not without help. An old shepherd with whom he served at Muckle Bein prayed with the lad and encouraged him in the religious life. He also encouraged him to continue with his books.

During a brief and broken career at the local school John Brown had been able to learn a little Latin. He went on with his studies himself, and made up his mind to learn Greek. There was no one to teach him, so he taught himself. Put like that it may sound difficult enough. But with almost no books it should have been impossible. However, having worked out the Greek alphabet by studying the proper names in Matthew I, he went on to discover the meaning of each word by comparing them with the English of the Bible. His method called for immense patience and uncommon linguistic ability. John Brown, it turned out, had both qualities.

These qualities produced one of the classic moments in the story of Scottish education. John Brown determined to have his own Greek testament. He saved hard and long. Then, with a friend looking after his sheep, he walked in his bare feet the 24 miles to St Andrews. He walked through the night and arrived the next morning. He found Alexander McCulloch's bookshop, went in and asked for a Greek testament. Some of the university staff were in the shop and looked up in surprise at the request of this barefoot lad of 16. One of them stepped forward. 'Boy,' he said, 'if you can read that book you shall have it for nothing.' And he did.

By now John Brown felt himself called to the ministry. There were a few other young men in the district who also wanted to be ministers, including William Moncrieff, the minister's son. Finding their own studies hard going they could not believe that this shepherd boy had mastered Greek. It was just not possible. But it was, and when they saw that he did know Greek some of them got upset. Somebody said, 'The devil must have taught you.' John Brown thought it was a joke. It proved to be very serious. Soon the word spread that the shepherd had made a pact with the devil, and sold his soul for learning. Some in and around Abernethy believed it, including the minister himself.

For five years John Brown was under a cloud. The kirk session would not give him a certificate of Church membership. So bad did things become that he left the district and travelled as a pedlar. He was something less than a total success at this, not

C

least because he confined his visits to houses and farms where the people had the name of being Christian. Moreover he could always forget his wares at the sight of a book. Folk were kind and he was well aware of their kindness. Yet the one thing he really wanted to do, the one thing he felt he was meant to do, seemed to be denied to him forever.

John Brown found comfort in his Bible. In particular, he said, Micah 7:7–10 came to mean a great deal. Here he found hope and strength to wait. And in the fulness of time the rest of these verses also came true, for John Brown lived to see some of his enemies shamed and downtrodden, a sight which gave him no pleasure, let it be said.

After service as a government soldier during the '45, and some time — very happily — as a school teacher, John Brown became an ordained minister. He was called to Haddington in 1751: 'The lad with the tattit heid,' said one old lady, 'there's a sweet savour of Christ about him.' At Haddington he established a sound reputation as a pastor and preacher. He was also known as a wise teacher; and his own denomination made him their professor. So to Haddington — once described by Jane Welsh Carlyle as 'the dimmest, deadest spot in the Creator's Universe' — came the Secession students and at the shepherd boy's feet they were glad to sit. Others, too, benefited from his learning. He wrote much, most notably his *Dictionary of the Bible* and his once-famous *Self-Interpreting Bible*, as well as a large number of tracts and pamphlets.

He also left behind a son and a grandson who would make their mark on Scottish life and letters, not to mention a famous great-grandson. He died in 1787, having served at Haddington for 36 years. His last words were 'my Christ'.

Those five years in the wilderness he never forgot. Rather, he learned not a few lessons from that bitter experience. And chiefly he learned the lesson taught by Micah the Prophet in chapter 7, verse 8, 'When I fall I shall rise; when I sit in darkness the Lord will be a light to me.'

Thomas Olivers
(1725–1799)

Zechariah 3:2

And the Lord said to Satan, 'The Lord rebuke you, O Satan! The Lord who has chosen Jerusalem rebuke you! Is not this a brand plucked from the fire?'

Do these conversions last? The question is still asked, just as it was then in the days when George Whitefield was travelling the country preaching to the crowds. This is the story of one of his converts.

Not that Thomas Olivers wanted to be a convert. Really it was only chance that he, a young ruffian who sometimes worked as a cobbler, should be in Bristol at the same time as Whitefield. He had been born, our Thomas, at Tregonan in Montgomeryshire. His parents had died when he was a child and he grew up with little education and less guidance. By the time he was 18 he had earned a reputation as a wild and reckless young man, a reputation of which he was rather proud. He took to a wandering life, working at his trade when he had to. Then one day he arrived in Bristol.

Naturally he had heard of George Whitefield. He had had many a laugh with his cronies about the mad preacher and his equally mad converts. So, hearing that the same Whitefield was in town and going to preach, Thomas set off to enjoy the show.

There is no doubt that he went in precisely this frame of mind. Nor is there any doubt as to what happened next. The sermon was on Zechariah 3:2, and before that sermon was over Thomas Olivers was a changed man. Years later he wrote, 'When the sermon started I was certainly a dreadful enemy to God and to all that is good,' but he says, 'By the time it was ended I was become a new creature.'

The change was sudden: just the length of a sermon made the difference. Yes, but was it real? Well, the first thing Thomas did afterwards was to go back to some of his old haunts and repay the debts he had left behind. There were, he says, 70 of them.

Then he joined John Wesley as a preacher. For the next 22 years he was on the road. Through England he went, into Scotland, over to Ireland. He once bought a horse at Tiverton. It cost him all of £5. But then it carried him some 100 000 miles. He travelled nearly as much as Wesley and spoke nearly as often. Not that Wesley was always pleased with his efforts. He once referred to him as 'a rough stick of wood', which was not meant as a compliment. But then Wesley had been disappointed with Thomas Olivers.

Perhaps it was his own fault. In 1775 Wesley appointed him supervisor of the Methodist Press. Thomas Olivers was then 50 but he was still no great scholar. The results might have been predicted. Publications were marred by many mistakes until they became, in Wesley's opinion, 'insufferable'. It also appears that poor Thomas was less than totally efficient as a supervisor, for articles somehow got into print without his passing them. So, after a number of years, he was quietly retired.

Yet Thomas Olivers had many gifts. If he was not a sucessful editor he could write. He wrote a number of hymns, composed at least one famous tune, and turned out many pamphlets. His best-known composition is the hymn 'The God of Abraham Praise'. This he wrote after hearing Meyer Leoni, a chorister in the Great Synagogue, singing the Yigdal. He wrote the words, borrowed the tune from Leoni, and presented it to the world as a tract. The hymn is particularly rich in biblical references and it meant a great deal to Henry Martyn (a famous missionary to India whose life, written by Wilberforce, was a major source of inspiration to many) at a difficult time in his life. It has meant much to many people since.

He also wrote a tune known as 'Helmsley' which has travelled a bit. This appears to be an adaptation from an old ballad which Thomas heard whistled in the street. He wrote it down and has thus been given the credit for its composition. It is said that Sheridan used the tune for one of his songs, but it is now forever associated with the hymn 'Lo! He comes, with clouds descending'.

It would have been quite fitting for the wandering preacher to have found his inspiration on the streets.

The change had been sudden. But it had been lasting and real. Thomas Olivers' faith was strong enough to take him into some very strange places and some very difficult situations. But it was also strong enough to carry him through them all. It gave him a message to preach, a song to sing, a life to live. He was indeed a brand plucked out of the fire.

Susan Warner
(1819–1885)

Matthew 5:15–16

Nor do men light a lamp and put it under a bushel, but on a stand, and it gives light to all in the house. [16]Let your light so shine before men, that they may see your good works and give glory to your Father who is in heaven.

No doubt there are various reasons why some writers favour the use of a pen-name. We do know that Mary Ann Evans became George Eliot, that Samuel Clemens turned into Mark Twain, that Neil Munro wrote his humourous sketches as Hugh Foulis, while John Creasey has employed at least 26 pseudonyms in his energetic career as a crime writer. And so on. To this list we should add the Warner sisters, Anna and Susan.

Susan Warner called herself Elizabeth Wetherell. Her young sister became Amy Lothrop. Both wrote and both were successful. This was important to them for they were quite definitely writing to make money.

Their father was a prominent lawyer of high character. This did not save him from disaster, and the family was threatened with ruin. So the two girls decided that they would keep the family together and the wolf from the door. They would do so, they said, by writing books. This, they were convinced, was their clear duty: to save the family by using the talents God had given them. Their best talent was their ability to tell a story.

In 1850 Susan's first book appeared. It was called *The Wide, Wide World*. Those critics who bothered to read it were not very impressed. It was a sentimental story about an orphan and that orphan's moral and religious progress. However, while critics sneered, the public bought and went on buying. The book went through 13 editions in two years, enjoying immense sales. It ran *Uncle Tom's Cabin* a very close second. It also was popular in other countries, being translated into French and German.

This was only the beginning. Other books followed: *Queechy* the next year, then *The Old Helmet*, *The Hills of the Shatemuc*, *Daisy* and many more. Without quite matching the success of the first one, these all proved popular.

There were other books, too. These were religious works, mainly for children as Susan Warner was particularly interested in children and older young people. From her home on Constitution Island in the Hudson River she would visit the Military Academy at West Point where for years she ran a Bible class for the cadets.

Anna was also hard at work. Her stories sold well too, *Dollars and Cents*, *My Brother's Keeper* and the rest. She also edited *Hymns of the Church Militant* in 1858 and 11 years later brought out another collection under the title *Wayfaring Hymns*. There were books on gardening and, later, a biography of her sister.

Anna took a share in the work among the cadets at West Point. Both were popular. In fact so close and harmonious was the relationship that they were both given military honours at their funerals.

Tastes change with the passing years. So it occasions no surprise to learn that the Warner novels, once so enormously popular, have been almost totally forgotten. The International Library of Famous Literature may have included a selection from *The Wide, Wide World* as late as 1900, but there has been little interest shown since then. The story of the sisters and their brave attempt to look after the family may also have been forgotten. However, there is one aspect of the sisters' work that has survived and kept their name alive. Both wrote hymns. Anna wrote 'Jesus loves me' and Susan gave the world 'Jesus bids us shine'.

Susan's hymn draws inspiration from Jesus' words as they are recorded in Matthew 5. The hymn reminds us that we can each do something to spread a little light in a dark world. Her own life was a commentary on that text. Finding her family threatened by darkness she lit the candle of her talent and by its light brought comfort and security to those she loved. She and Anna made their small corner brighter and in so doing they helped others to find their way more easily through the darkness.

John Owen
(1616–1683)

Matthew 8:26

And he said to them, 'Why are you afraid, O men of little faith?'
Then he rose and rebuked the winds and the sea; and there was a
great calm.

He was a personal friend of Oliver Cromwell. Yet his opinion was
sought by the king. The Americans wanted him to be President of
Harvard. And he was for a time Vice-Chancellor of Oxford. He
was invited to preach before the House of Commons. And he
wrote books that are still in print today, 300 years on.

His name was John Owen. And he owed his life to that text
from Matthew 8. While still a boy he had gone to Oxford University. There he had worked at a fearful pace, making do most
nights with only four hours' sleep. He took his degrees, of course.
But at a price. The pressure of such intense study caught up with
him. John Owen became ill. His nerves gave way. Now he was a
religious young man, but at this time his religion brought him no
comfort. It seemed only to increase his anxiety and deepen his
depression. It cost him in other ways too. A rich uncle in Wales
was going to leave him an estate until he heard of young John's
religion — and that was the end of that. When the English Civil
War broke out he lost his job and came to London where some
relations took him in.

One Sunday his cousin invited him to come to church. They
would go to hear the famous preacher Dr Edmund Calamy.
Crowds came to hear Calamy. John and his cousin only just got
in. And then the wrong man came into the pulpit! Not Dr
Calamy, but a stranger. Someone from the country. A nobody.
Some of the people got up to leave. The cousin got up. But John
was too tired to move. He just could not be bothered. So he sat
on.

And he heard the stranger's sermon on Matthew 8:26. There
was nothing fancy about it, just a plain ordinary sermon, delivered

with no special style. But it went straight to John Owen's heart. He was fearful, and had been so for years; his fears haunted him and he couldn't get rid of them. But that sermon, that simple sermon, gave him the answer. He was fearful because, like the disciples in the boat out on the lake, he had forgotten who was with him. John Owen had tried to face life alone and it was too big for him. He had tried to find peace with God, but God had seemed too far away. Now he saw that Jesus was there, had always been there. And Jesus was there not to judge and condemn, but to save and to help. In that sermon John Owen found Jesus. And John Owen found peace and strength.

There were plenty of storms to face after that. But John Owen was no longer alone, and he faced them all. He was, in fact, a very brave man. For, while he was a friend of Cromwell and acted as his chaplain in Ireland and Scotland, he wasn't afraid to tell Cromwell when he thought him wrong. Later on, when Charles II wanted his advice, and Owen knew what the king wanted to hear, he told him the truth instead. Clear and to the point he was too. Owen lost various posts at different times because he insisted on taking a stand, but he never hesitated to stand up and speak out.

John Owen was one of the leading controversialists of the day, turning out pamphlets and books in great number. However, he was also a very fair man, and unusually tolerant for those days. For example, when he was at Oxford he made sure that vacant posts went to the best men, whatever their brand of churchmanship. While he was always ready to defend his own views and to oppose error wherever he saw it, he was a great believer in religious freedom. That was unusual then. And it's not so common now either.

Owen worked hard all his days. In later years his health was none too good; in particular he suffered much from asthma, but he kept on going. He was still in the boat, out in the rough waters, but now he knew that Jesus was with him, and — amid all the storms — there was peace in his heart.

He never did find out who had preached that sermon that changed his life. He tried to discover the identity of the preacher. But he never did. In a way that's a pity, for it's not hard to imagine how much it would have meant to some obscure country minister, tempted perhaps to imagine that he had never achieved anything worth while, to hear that under his preaching John

Owen had been led to peace. Surely two lessons are to be learned here by any preacher: the first is that we never know who in the congregation might be needing a particular word, but there is One who does know, and, the second lesson, let it be remembered that this is his Word. So let us pray that the Word might go forth with all its ancient power whenever his people gather.

Annie S Swan
(1859–1943)

Matthew 10:42

And whoever gives to one of these little ones even a cup of cold water because he is a disciple, truly, I say to you, he shall not lose his reward.

They finally met some years later in a London drawing room. She was able to thank him for his cup of cold water. That is how Annie Swan described it, as a cup of cold water. She remembered that day very vividly.

She had been tired. She was often tired then, tired and dispirited. She certainly could not face church that morning; for once the thought of all those friendly faces was too much. They would ask her how she was. They would be kind in their enquiries she knew, but just then the last thing she wanted was kindness. She wanted to be alone. So she went for a walk in Hyde Park.

After walking for some time Annie found that her steps had taken her to Portman Square. St Paul's Church was open and the congregation was going in. She really was tired now. She had to sit down. So she went in and sat down near the door. No one had recognised her. She could be quiet here.

The preacher began his sermon. Annie did not know him and he did not know her. She was quite definite about that. It made what happened next all the more surprising. His sermon somehow spoke to her condition and was as refreshing as a drink of fresh cold water. It was, she said, a definite message to Annie Swan, and it brought her an immense comfort. Somehow his words told her exactly what she needed to hear. She left St Paul's happy and strong.

To most folk Annie Swan was happy and strong. They knew that she was a very successful writer. Her books were in all the shops. She wrote for *The People's Friend* and she even had her 'own' magazine, *The Woman at Home*. Her serials were followed avidly, even anxiously. She just had to be rich. And was she not married to the nice Doctor Smith? Of course she was happy. What else could she be? Life had been good to Annie Swan.

Annie Swan, however, had had to work very hard to gain this success. And her life had had its share of sorrows. Her father, a potato merchant, had been a good man without being a good man of business. So at times there had been money and the family had lived in some comfort. But then there had been other times. Annie's mother had died after a long illness and a year later the father had remarried. The step-mother had been difficult to live with and one by one the children had left home. No, the early years had not been without some sadness.

Annie married a schoolmaster. This schoolmaster, however, had ambitions to be a doctor. Those first years of married life, spent at the little schoolhouse of Star near Markinch, were happy. They were also poor. So they came to a decision, this young couple. He would go to university and become a doctor. She would keep them both through her writing. It was a bold step to take. Annie was only beginning to make a name for herself and so had no secure future. Undaunted, they moved to Edinburgh, where they struggled.

Things were not easy. Often there was not enough food to eat. The family did not help much, nor did most of their friends. 'Perfect nonsense,' her father had cried when they told him their plans. Others shook their heads at a man who was prepared to let his wife keep him at university. These were hard days to come through.

Hard, too, was the sorrow when their son Ned had an accident while packing for school at the end of the holidays. He was putting a gun away when it went off. He died within half an hour. The father, who had bought the gun, was devastated and, on top of her own grief, Annie had the anxiety of his broken health. No, life was not always kind to Annie Swan.

The First World War added to her troubles. Her husband insisted on going out to France and their daughter Effie, although under age, went out to work with the YMCA. The family home at Hertford was destroyed in a Zeppelin raid, although no one was hurt. As a well-known personality, Annie too was involved in the war effort. She went to visit troops in France and she made the hazardous Atlantic crossing to tour the United States. There she had to deal with indifferent officialdom and hostile audiences. She met the challenge bravely and her work in America proved most successful as she brought home to the people there the gravity of the situation and the horror of war.

Hers was a busy life. A life with its share of worry and sadness. No wonder then that Annie Swan appreciated that cup of cold water. The Church had always been a big thing in her life, right from her childhood Sundays at a tiny Evangelical Union church in Leith. She always went to church and, she said, she always found help. 'Every church is my Father's house where, if sought in humility and faith, he can be found.'

Annie Swan heard some of the most famous preachers of the day. She was friendly with Dr Joseph Parker of the City Temple whose friendship she valued highly. Yet Portman Square, its unknown preacher, and his cup of cold water, she never forgot. That cup not only refreshed her then, the memory of it stayed with her and cheered her on many occasions. It also encouraged her to do what she could to help others.

Susan Ferrier
(1782–1854)

Matthew 25:36

I was naked and you clothed me, I was sick and you visited me, I was in prison and you came to me.

Susan Ferrier liked to talk. Sir Walter Scott confided in his journal that in conversation she was 'simple, full of humour, and exceedingly ready at repartee'. And, he added, 'all this without the least affectation of the blue stocking'.

Scott knew her very well. Her father was James Ferrier, a principal Clerk of Session. In fact Ferrier had helped Scott secure a position as clerk by persuading an old colleague to retire in Scott's favour. Ferrier himself was on the best of good terms with the leading men in the literary society of Edinburgh. Susan, the youngest of his ten children, grew up in a world of books and bookmen.

Some time in 1810 she began to write. It started as something of a game. Susan and her close friend, Charlotte Clavering, decided to write a novel. At first they intended to share the writing but very soon Susan took over, while Charlotte became her critic and advisor. There was no hurry to finish the book as they had no idea of publishing it. Until, that is, Maria Edgeworth came on the scene. Her stories of Irish life enjoyed great popularity and helped change the public taste. She proved that there was a market for simple stories of everyday life — and that a woman could write a good book.

On top of this there was the appearance of the *Waverley* novels. Their success established a vogue for Scottish tales. So Susan Ferrier finished her book, called it *Marriage*, and saw it published in 1818. She wrote two more books, *The Inheritance*, which appeared in 1824, and *Destiny* in 1831. All were successful and there was considerable discussion as to which of the three was the best. There was also considerable discussion as to the writer's identity, for Susan had refused to let her name appear. It is interesting to learn that some experts insisted that Scott — but recently revealed as the author of *Waverley* — was the writer.

Scott himself was a sincere admirer of her books. When, for example, he wrote his postscript to *A Legend of Montrose*, in which he said he would write no more Scottish stories, he told his readers that this work would be continued by some younger writers of whom the most promising was the author of *Marriage*. He also admitted quite cheerfully that there were some books that women could write better than any mere man.

They were thus old friends, liking each other and admiring each other's work. Who better, then, to help Scott during his years of ill health than Miss Ferrier? Susan had never married, she had kept house for her father after her mother's death, and then — when he died and she was 47 — she set herself up in her own home on the road to Morningside. She was a frequent visitor at Abbotsford.

However, it is one thing to visit the sick. It is quite another to do it well. Susan did it well.

In 1831 she was invited to Abbotsford by Scott's daughters. They knew their father would be pleased to see her and they hoped that she might even tempt him out of his study. Despite his failing health Scott was still struggling to write another book, and the family was deeply concerned about the effect of such strain. They were also worried that the meeting might after all go badly. Sir Walter liked to talk, although his speech was slurred, but he was often unable to complete what he was saying. He seemed to lose his way, and this upset him greatly. He would be sure to talk to his old friend but he was certain to have one of these lapses and the family was afraid how it would affect him.

Susan Ferrier solved the problem with great delicacy and kindliness. She pretended to have grown a little deaf; her eyesight was actually failing although her hearing was good. Whenever Scott lost the thread of his story she would apologise and say, 'Well, I am getting as deaf as a post; I have not heard a word since you said so and so,' and she would mention the last thing he had said. This not only let him pick up his discourse, it saved him any embarrassment. He quite believed her and forgot his own disability.

Susan Ferrier's books are still read. Her humour still makes people smile. However, her best work was done while visiting her sick friend and bringing a little sunshine into a dark corner.

Beatrice Clugston
(1827–1888)

Matthew 25:40

And the King will answer them, 'Truly, I say to you, as you did it to one of the least of these my brethren, you did it to me.'

Beatrice Clugston looked out at the distinguished gathering. James White of Overtoun was in the chair. Sir Peter Coates was there, James Campbell of Tillechewan Castle, Mr Holms the Member of Parliament ... so many others. She would not keep them long. When her turn to speak came she said she had only to thank them for their generosity. As for her services, which they were so kindly recognising, she had but done her best — a poor best — to serve the Master and his children. Her reward, she told them, would be to hear him say the words of Matthew 25:40.

Beatrice Clugston was born in the east end of the city of Glasgow. Her father, a power loom manufacturer and bleacher, was active in many local charitable efforts and her mother was also always ready to help. Beatrice grew up believing that helping others was the main business of life. It was to be the main business of her life.

But there were so many to help! Visiting the Royal Infirmary she uncovered two areas of concern that had gone largely undetected. Patients, she found, were often anxious about the welfare of their families and this impeded their recovery. So, in response to their fears, she took it upon herself to visit the homes of patients and to see how things were. It quickly became obvious that this work was far too heavy for any one person. So she set out to find other helpers, something that Beatrice was to become very good at doing.

The second problem she found was that many patients simply did not have adequate clothes or proper shoes in which to return home. Once again Beatrice tried to fill the gap and, once again, she soon learned the wisdom of involving others. A small clothing store was opened in the hospital; at first she financed this herself.

Soon, however, she had organised others in the work. From these personal enterprises the Royal Infirmary Dorcas Society was formed.

About this time — the early 1870s — Beatrice and her mother moved house to Lenzie. Their new home in the country gave her another idea. She knew that many patients had to leave hospital before they were anything like fit enough to return to their daily lives. A rest after hospitalisation was needed. So, once more, Beatrice got busy and a little later the Glasgow Convalescent Home was opened in Bothwell.

Her scheme proved too successful: a bigger home was needed. Two farms were then bought outside Lenzie and Lord Shaftesbury came to lay the foundation stone. Within two years the doors were opened and the first patients admitted. She had worked hard behind the scenes to enlist help and had involved the leading citizens of Glasgow from the planning stage. The general public got their chance to help when a mammoth bazaar was held to raise funds. This, too, became a feature of her work.

Much as the people appreciated the fresh air of the country, it was the sea air of the coast that appealed most strongly at this time. Trips 'doon the watter' were considered essential. Where better, then, to open the next home than at Dunoon on the Clyde coast? And why not bring in the working men of Glasgow from the beginning this time and give them a more prominent part in the fund-raising?

Beatrice's idea proved a winner. Within four months of the first meeting, house and grounds had been purchased and another four months saw the first 90 patients arrive. The work at Dunoon continued to expand and by the turn of the century some 300 beds were available.

Now another concern moved Beatrice Clugston. She had seen how society neglected the incurably ill, so once more she set to work, rousing interest, organising help. A society was again formed, the Association for the Relief of Incurables, the first of its kind in the country. Funds were raised — a bazaar in the Kibble Palace brought in £14 000 — and once more a home was created, the Broomhill Home near Kirkintilloch. This, it was agreed, was her greatest triumph. It had been hard work convincing society that incurables should be helped. After all, they were by definition incurable, they would never be able to become really useful members of the community, so why make such a fuss over them?

Beatrice remembered the words of Matthew: it was a hard job but one that had to be done. And it was.

There was, of course, a price to be paid. She had never hesitated to use her own money to support her causes. She had gone on spending when that money was almost exhausted, making no provision for her own declining years. This time she needed help. Hence the meeting in Glasgow, the presentation, the speeches. Yet even here there was thought for others. Those who had arranged the gift had done so privately. Now that the presentation was public knowledge, it was said that anyone else who felt moved to do something should send their gifts not to Beatrice Clugston but to the homes.

They found her one summer morning in 1888 kneeling in prayer beside her bed. She did not need any help now. She had by then already heard her Master speak those words that had been her inspiration.

Ed 'Strangler' Lewis
(1890–1966)

Mark 8:36

For what does it profit a man, to gain the whole world and forfeit his life?

William Hazlitt got it right. 'Of all eloquence,' he wrote, 'a nickname is the most concise: of all arguments the most unanswerable.' Even when it is borrowed. Robert Frederick did just that. When he dropped out of college to follow his new career he took not only Evan Lewis' surname, he also commandeered his nickname: 'Strangler'.

There was a good reason for this choice of name. The original Lewis had been a well-known professional wrestler and a professional wrestler was what young Robert Frederick wanted to be. Not only that, but the farm boy from Wisconsin had already developed his own particular head lock and 'Strangler' was a perfect description. The name didn't hurt his publicity either.

In 1914 Lewis first broke into the big time when he won a major tournament in New York. In 1920 he took the world title from Joe Stetcher, in a three-hour bout. For the next 13 years or so Lewis dominated the sport. True, he sometimes lost his title but he always won it again. He was champion some five times. Unquestionably he was the best known wrestler in the world. Some would say he was the best professional wrestler ever. Period.

Lewis in fact won a new audience for the game and in doing so he became a rich man. He had a lot of fun spending the money too. He was popular with the public and admired by his fellow professionals. He had everything he had ever wanted. So why did he feel like jumping into the sea? Ed 'Strangler' Lewis, champion of the world, the man who had everything, and here he was, returning from a triumphant tour of Europe, standing at the rail of the ship, wanting to end it all.

He had felt like this before; never quite as badly as now, but this sense of emptiness was always there. Sometimes it made him miserable, sometimes it made him angry, but it never seemed to leave him. He had an ulcer. Imagine that, the strongest man in the world, and he had given himself an ulcer. What was wrong with him?

Well, he didn't jump. He came back to America and went on the road again. He was still unhappy. No one else knew how unhappy. Then one afternoon in Cleveland he found the answer.

He saw a shoe-shine boy. A happy shoe-shine boy. He was poor, his clothes were in rags. He had no right to be happy, yet happy he most certainly was. He was content. That was it, he was content. The discovery shook Lewis. This shoe-shine boy had something that he, with all his success, did not have. What was missing?

Lewis took a hard look at himself. He had everything, he had gained the whole world. Yet he was not a crude strong man with no sensitivity. Lewis was something of a thinker and he liked to believe that he had not neglected his mental development while building up his body. He was living what most folk would consider a very full life. Yet, confronted by that happy shoe-shine boy, he knew that something was missing.

And then he saw, with frightening clarity, that in his full and busy life he had forgotten God. There had been no place for religion, no time. He had made his mark on the world, but had he lost his soul?

Lewis took his anxieties and his hopes to a friend. Talking it over, asking and listening, Lewis found his answer. With his new faith there came a new peace. Lewis always insisted that, when converted, his 'body chemistry changed too'.

Lewis' declining years were not without problems. The money had disappeared and his sight had failed. He suffered from trachoma, a disease of the eye once common among wrestlers, which had hit him first in his championship days. He had recovered his sight then and had said that his new faith had helped him in his recovery. When he went blind the second time he was in his 70s and was told that there was no possibility that he would regain his sight. Could his faith help him now? Lewis was hopeful that he would see again, but even in his blindness he could say, 'I am going through a beautiful experience. This is just another test to prove God's allness. I have gained in spirit. I have acquired a true sense of human values.' And in that confidence the old wrestler fought out the good fight to the final bell.

Charles Kingsley
(1819–1875)

Mark 11:24

Therefore I tell you, whatever you ask in prayer, believe that you receive it, and you will.

The trouble with doing something clever is that some people want you to do it again. That's what happened to Charles Kingsley. He wrote a children's book — *The Heroes* — and he dedicated it to his three children (Rose, Maurice, and Mary). This was fine. Especially as the book was a great success. But then a few years later, after the arrival of another boy (Grenville Arthur), Kingsley's wife said to him that as the other three had their book 'the baby must have his'. Of course, it was a joke. But there and then Kingsley got up from the breakfast table, went to his study, and locked the door. Half an hour later he came out again with the first chapter of a new book. The story was written very quickly, serialised in a magazine that year, and published as a book the next. It was called *The Water Babies*.

It was an even greater success. It is still a popular children's book today. It is also a book that changed the law of the land, and did so within a year.

The story, you may remember, is about an orphan boy, called Tom, who is employed by the cruel Mr Grimes to climb chimneys. It's a strange story that can be read at several levels, but it had such an impact when it first appeared that a law was passed that year to stop the use of boy chimney sweeps. Other people were campaigning against that evil trade too, of course, but this book, this children's book, made the difference.

The same thing happened with another of his stories. This was an adult novel, *Alton Locke*, which exposed conditions in the clothing industry in London's East End. In particular, it showed what happens to people when they have no pure drinking water. Within a short time of the book's publication, piped water was supplied to that district.

Charles Kingsley wrote a lot. He was a minister, a country minister who served all his life in the small Hampshire village of Eversley. His books were part of his work. 'If I have wrapped up my parable in seeming tomfooleries, it is because so only could I get the pill swallowed by this generation.' In other words, Kingsley had something to say and he realised that this was one way to say it. People who would not hear a sermon, who would ignore a tract, would listen to a story. And he knew how to tell them a story.

Charles Kingsley was a great campaigner. He believed that if Christianity is real, it must be visible, it must be seen to make a difference. In his society there was much that needed to be changed and Kingsley believed passionately that Christians had to be involved in bringing about those changes. Sometimes it didn't work out. In an early attempt to provide Londoners with fresh water he had barrels supplied to every street corner in one of the worst districts. Each day they would be filled with clean water. At least that was the plan. The very first night all the barrels were stolen.

Like everyone who tries to help people, Kingsley was sometimes misunderstood. In his early days this deeply religious man was called a communist — they used the word then. He didn't like that, but he didn't allow it to stop him from trying again. Naturally, there were times when he did feel like giving up, letting someone else take on the work. There were times when he got tired and dispirited. There were even times when his health broke down under the strain. He took that badly for he had always been something of a fitness fanatic.

But there he was, in his prime, a strong, brave, generous man — very much a man's man — putting his faith into practice and, shrugging off disappointments, ever ready to tackle a new problem. To see him then, to hear him then, you'd never imagine the bad time he once came through.

While studying at Cambridge he decided not to pursue the career in law that he had been contemplating. He felt he had to be a minister. This, he believed, was now his place in life, the area where he could do most good, the place where God wanted him to be. So he came to Eversley as an assistant, and he got engaged to be married. And that's when the trouble started.

Kingsley knew that he couldn't remain an assistant. He had to move on. But where? When? How? He couldn't marry until he was settled in a parish. But what if he never got settled? It seemed as if no one wanted him. Here he was, young and eager and all the doors seemed closed. It began to get him down. The longer it went on the worse it got. After some months he even stopped writing to his fiancée. He no longer knew what to say; he couldn't see any way out.

And then this verse spoke to him. Kingsley had read the text before. Often. But it never hit him as it did now. It was as if Jesus himself was talking to him, for these are his own words, this is his promise. Kingsley now saw that if he had been called to this work then God had a plan for him, God had a place for him. Where it was and when it would come he still did not know. But now he knew that his future was in the best hands of all. And with that knowledge his peace of mind returned. 'Mark 11:24 saved me from madness in my 12 months sorrows.'

How Kingsley came to Eversley as parish minister was something no one could have foreseen. The minister there, a real rascal, suddenly cleared off leaving the church vacant. The people let it be known that they wanted their assistant to take over the work. Again there was an agonising delay as everyone waited to see who would be appointed. Then the one job of work he most wanted was given to Kingsley.

Certainly there were other difficulties he had to face and there were times when the doubts would creep back. But something happened to Kingsley during that 12-month wait. He learned a great secret: he discovered from that text in Mark that the future is safe because it is in the hands of the Master. If we want to serve him and to do his work, he will find a place for us, and it will be the right place. For it will be where he wants us to be.

Charlotte Elliott
(1789–1871)

Luke 9:23

And he said to all, 'If any man would come after me, let him deny himself and take up his cross daily and follow me.'

Clapham was then little more than a village. Some three miles outside London, it had a population of about 1000. But it had a reputation all of its own, on account of some rather well-known people who lived there. They were sometimes called the Clapham Sect. They were prominent Christian activists: men such as William Wilberforce, James Stephen, Charles Grant, all famous for the part they took in public life. They all went to the same church, and they all sat under the same preacher, John Venn.

In that same congregation was a young woman called Charlotte Elliott. She came from a very religious family; her grandfather had been a much-loved minister, and she grew up in an atmosphere of church services and family prayers. She also grew up surrounded by preachers. She was quite used to visiting ministers staying at the family home. Until, that is, Dr Caesar Malan arrived from Geneva.

He had been there a few days when he suddenly asked Charlotte if he might speak to her in private. When they were alone he asked another question, one that shocked and angered her. 'Are you,' he asked, 'a Christian?' She was deeply offended. How dare he ask her such a thing! What business was it of his? Was she a Christian indeed! How could he possibly think she was anything else? Didn't he know that she went to church, that she listened to Mr Venn, that she loved the music? What did he mean, are you a Christian?

Charlotte told him to mind his own business. He apologised. But then said he would pray for her. That was almost as bad as his question. Poor Charlotte was upset. But somehow she couldn't get his question out of her mind. Was she a Christian? What did it mean to be a Christian? Was it something more than she had imagined, was it something she did not have?

A fortnight later she found Dr Malan in the garden. This time she was first to speak. She approached him and she asked him what it meant to be a Christian. He looked at her and quietly asked, 'Have you ever come to Christ?' She knew then what he meant and she knew the answer to his question too. 'I would like to come,' she said, 'but I don't know how.' 'Young lady,' he replied, 'don't worry. Come to him just as you are.'

That day in the garden altered everything. Up until then Charlotte's religion had been a matter of form. It didn't go very deep. Yes, she had known all about Jesus, she knew the story, but she had never until then known Jesus. But she did as the doctor ordered. She came to Jesus as she was — 'with many a conflict, many a doubt' — and she found that she was accepted. She discovered that Jesus loved Charlotte Elliott. And she felt a peace she had never known before.

The story doesn't stop here. In fact this is really only the beginning. Having found the love of Jesus herself, Charlotte now felt that she had to share her knowledge, helping others to find it too. But how? It was all right for her brother. He was a minister. He could preach every Sunday. He could spread the good news every day. But she was a woman, and a sick one at that. She really hadn't been well for years. She was in truth little better than an invalid. What could she do?

She thought of one thing. She had always been fond of writing. Even as a child she had been good with words, and had a talent for verse. Here was something she could do. So Charlotte Elliott began to write: she wrote hymns. Some of our best-loved hymns came from her pen.

There was an unexpected sequel. People wrote to Charlotte, to tell her how much she had helped them. After her death they found a box among her possessions. When they opened it they discovered inside over a thousand letters, all from people who had been helped by her verses. How that must have helped her.

You see, it was never easy for Charlotte. Every single day she had to fight off pain and weakness and make herself write. She once said how easy it would have been to give in, to lie down and feel sorry for herself, to get angry at the unfairness of it all. Yes, how easy to grow bitter and selfish and lazy. Every day she felt she had to battle against all those feeling. But she tells us how she did it. She gave herself a motto which she repeated every morning. The road was long; for 50 years she was an invalid, and it was often rough. But it was the Master's road, the way he went. And he walked it still. That gave her courage.

This saying of Jesus is given by Matthew and Mark as well as Luke, but Charlotte preferred Luke's version, because Luke keeps in one word that the other two let slip. Let a man take up his cross, they all say. But Luke adds let him take it up daily. Charlotte Elliott knew what that meant. It was something she had to do. Daily. But she shows how it can be done. And what blessing that brings to others.

Elizabeth Clephane
(1830–1869)

Luke 15:1–7

Now the tax collectors and sinners were all drawing near to hear him. [2]And the Pharisees and the scribes murmured, saying, 'This man receives sinners and eats with them.'

[3]So he told them this parable: [4]'What man of you, having a hundred sheep, if he has lost one of them, does not leave the ninety-nine in the wilderness, and go after the one which is lost, until he finds it? [5]And when he has found it, he lays it on his shoulders, rejoicing. [6]And when he comes home, he calls together his friends and his neighbours, saying to them, 'Rejoice with me, for I have found my sheep which was lost.' [7]Just so, I tell you, there will be more joy in heaven over one sinner who repents than over ninety-nine righteous persons who need no repentance.

The three sisters lived together, as they had always done. First in their parents' home in Edinburgh. A rather fine place it was, too, for their father was the Sheriff Principal of Fife and Kinross, a man of some importance. When he died the family moved to the village of Ormiston in East Lothian. Then, when the mother died, they moved again, this time to a house outside Melrose. Bridgend House it was called and it stands where the Ellwyn Water joins the Tweed.

There were brothers in the family too. The oldest of these, George, went to Canada. Hopes were high that he would do well. But he was young, and easily led and things went very wrong. He died in poverty and disgrace before he was 33.

Word came back to Scotland. They were all upset. The youngest of the girls, Elizabeth, barely 21, went to her room and shut the door. She wanted to be alone. But she also needed to give vent to her feelings. She sat down at her desk, took up her pen and began to write. She put her thoughts down on paper. And what she wrote was a poem, a poem of hope. Her hope for her brother, the lost sheep. Her hope that the shepherd had found him in time.

She locked that poem away. She had written it for herself, to relieve her feelings. She didn't want anyone else to see it. It wasn't for them.

In the town she and her sisters were already well-known. They were, all three of them, members of the Free Church there and they were all active and enthusiastic members. They had decided that anything they had — and it wasn't all that much — had been given them to be used. And used in the Master's work. So they gave generously to their church.

The church treasurer would be asked to call at their house at the end of each year. Although they themselves had given all through the year, they wanted to know if there was a deficit. And, if there was, they would pay it. And if they didn't have the money, they would sell something, and pay it then.

But it didn't stop there. They themselves went visiting. They got to know the town and the surrounding district. Here and there, when their kindly eyes saw need of any kind, they would help. Quietly. Always quietly. And always with a smile. Especially Elizabeth.

That's why they called her 'the Sunbeam'; she brightened many a dark corner. Melrose was no slum city, but it did have its poor, its old and its sick. Elizabeth gave herself to them. She herself was not very strong, and didn't live long. But the time she had she used to do good. Like her Master.

She did a bit of writing too, for she had always been good with words. Her cousin ran a paper for children — *The Children's Hour* it was called — and Elizabeth would write pieces for it. This time the cousin called for a contribution at short notice. Of course she was sorry to do so, she knew it was unfair, but who else could help? Elizabeth gave her a poem. A poem she had written and locked away years before. A poem about a lost sheep, and a good shepherd. A year later Elizabeth died but her story was not over.

One afternoon in May 1874 the two famous American evangelists, Dwight Moody and Ira Sankey were on a train heading from Glasgow to Edinburgh. Sankey was looking through a paper he had bought at the station. He wasn't finding much to interest him when his eye was caught by a poem. It struck him as rather special. So he cut it out and put it in his pocket. Then, with all the excitement of arriving and going to the rally at the Assembly Hall, he forgot all about it. The hall was full. Moody, the preacher, was magnificent. He had a magnificent message — about the Good Shepherd who lays down his life for the sheep. As he finished he turned to Sankey, the singer, and asked him for a hymn, something to fit in with the sermon and bring its message home. And suddenly Sankey remembered that poem. It was, he said later, as if a voice told him, 'Sing the words you found today, the poem on the train.' He took out the cutting. He had no music prepared, but an old Negro spiritual came back to him and he began to sing:

> There were ninety and nine that safely lay
> In the shelter of the fold;
> But one was out on the hills away,
> Far off from the gates of gold;
> Away on the mountains wild and bare,
> Away from the tender Shepherd's care.

The words were those written by Elizabeth Clephane, the words she wrote out of her own tragic loss, out of her own deep sorrow. The hope that lifted her then has, through her, lifted thousands. That hymn has been sung everywhere. And it never fails to touch some heart.

> Lord, whence are these blood drops all the way,
> That mark out the mountain's track?
> They were shed for one who had gone astray,
> Ere the Shepherd could bring him back.
> Lord, whence are Thy hands so rent and torn?
> They are pierced tonight by many a thorn.

As she wrote she was thinking of her own brother far from home. She was thinking of the love of Jesus, the Good Shepherd, who seeks and finds the lost. So, even in her sorrow, she can close with the hope that wins over fear:

> Rejoice, for the Lord brings back His own.

Elizabeth knew the love of Jesus. And it not only brought her peace. It made her the Sunbeam.

John Welsh
(c 1570–1622)

Luke 15:11–32

And he said, 'There was a man who had two sons; [12]and the younger of them said to his father, "Father, give me the share of property that falls to me." And he divided his living between them. [13]Not many days later, the younger son gathered all he had and took his journey into a far country, and there he squandered his property in loose living. [14]And when he had spent everything, a great famine arose in that country, and he began to be in want. [15]So he went and joined himself to one of the citizens of that country, who sent him into his fields to feed swine. [16]And he would gladly have fed on the pods that the swine ate; and no one gave him anything. [17]But when he came to himself he said, "How many of my father's hired servants have bread enough and to spare, but I perish here with hunger. [18]I will arise and go to my father, and I will say to him, 'Father, I have sinned against heaven and before you; [19]I am no longer worthy to be called your son; treat me as one of your hired servants.'" [20]And he arose and came to his father. But while he was yet at a distance, his father saw him and had compassion, and ran and embraced him and kissed him. [21]And the son said to him, "Father, I have sinned against heaven and before you; I am no longer worthy to be called your son." [22]But the father said to his servants, "Bring quickly the best robe, and put it on him; and put a ring on his hand, and shoes on his feet; [23]and bring the fatted calf and kill it, and let us eat and make merry; [24]for this my son was dead, and is alive again; he was lost, and is found." And they began to make merry.

[25]Now his elder son was in the field; and as he came and drew near to the house, he heard music and dancing. [26]And he called one of the servants and asked what this meant. [27]And he said to him, "Your brother has come, and your father has killed the fatted calf, because he has received him safe and sound." [28]But he was angry and refused to go in. His father came out and entreated him, [29]but he answered his father. "Lo, these many years I have served you, and I never disobeyed your command; yet you never gave me a kid, that I might make merry with my friends. [30]But when this son of yours came, who has devoured your living with harlots, you killed for him the fatted calf!" [31]And he said to him, "Son, you are always with me, and all that is mine is yours. [32]It was fitting to make merry and be glad, for this your brother was dead, and is alive; he was lost, and is found."

You can see it yourself in the High Street of Ayr. Always assuming you know where to look, and the hurrying shoppers don't knock you over while you are looking. But there it is, a small bronze-coloured plaque, on the bank building next to a big store. It tells us that near this spot stood the garden of John Welsh, adding that he was a minister in the town way back in the early 1600s. That's a long time ago. Who should anyone remember him today? And why should his garden be of any interest?

John Welsh was a prodigal son. We all know that story, know it very well. But, if we're honest, have we not sometimes wondered, was the father right? Should he have forgiven the prodigal so easily? What if he went back, this son, and did it all again? Do people really change?

Jesus, of course, told the story to show us what God is like. God is like the father. And he does forgive us when we don't deserve it. And, when we think about that, really think, we're very glad that he does.

But that other question, about people like this really changing. Well, let me introduce John Welsh. As a young man he ran away from home. He had got in with a bad crowd, and off he went. It was going to be fun. He was going to have a great time. Only — like the prodigal — it didn't quite work out. Before long the great adventure had turned sour. John Welsh wanted to go home. He was sorry now, and he realised what a fool he had been. But he was afraid to return. So he went instead to an aunt of his who lived in Dumfries. And there one day, all unexpected, his father turned up. The aunt spoke up. The father listened. John was brought in. And, as in the parable, the prodigal was taken home.

John Welsh promised his father that he wouldn't let him down again. He was a changed person, he said. And, he added, he had found faith. Now lots of people talk like that when they're caught. They promise all sorts of things. 'Just give me another chance . . .'

Well, John got his other chance. And he took it because he was changed. He had found faith. The next time he left home it was to go to Edinburgh University, as a student for the ministry. He studied hard, passed his exams, and came out to preach. First in Selkirk. Then in Kirkcudbright. And then, in the year 1600, he came to Ayr.

It must be admitted that the folk of Ayr didn't like him. They already had a minister, an old, easy-going kind of minister. They didn't take to this new kind at all; he was far too eager and he took everything far too seriously. Ayr at this time was a wild place; 'the wicked old town' people called it. In particular the town was famous far and wide for the fighting that disturbed its narrow streets every time certain families met. The old minister had kept well away. Not John Welsh. He plunged right in, and before anyone quite knew what had happened, the fighting stopped. Folk who had been fierce enemies became firm friends because of Welsh. There was something about the man that made folk listen to him. And they had ample opportunity to listen, for Welsh preached every day. But they did listen. People were changed by what they heard. The whole town became a different place.

So much so that when Welsh was sent into exile in France, the folk not only wrote to him, they not only went to visit him, they also went on paying his stipend. But what's this about exile in France? Why was Welsh sent away? Because he dared to speak out against the changes the king was trying to impose on the Church. Welsh defended the freedom of the Church and was put in prison for his trouble. When that didn't quieten him, he — and some others — were banished from Scotland for life.

It tells us a lot about the man that he made the best of this. He learned French and became a minister over there. He went on speaking up for the freedom of the Church and got himself into even more trouble. Some time find out what John Welsh said to the King of France. And what his wife said to the King of England.

Yes, the change had been real, and lasting. John Welsh had found forgiveness, from his father and from his Father. That is what changed him. Having seen the love of God in his own life, he just had to show that love to others. He was a man with a message and nothing would stop him telling that message.

The garden played a big part in his life. John spent hours there every day, praying. His garden was a quiet place where he could be alone with his Master. Once, in his early years, he had wandered away. Jesus had led him back. Now he would stay close. The prodigal came home — to stay.

Jemima Luke
(1813–1906)

Luke 18:16

But Jesus called them to him, saying, 'Let the children come to me, and do not hinder them; for to such belongs the kingdom of God.'

It was a beautiful spring morning when Miss Thompson set out. The stage-coach picked her up and she sat back to enjoy the journey. She knew it would take an hour or so to reach the town of Wellington. There was no one else inside the coach; that made everything perfect. Miss Thompson took out an old envelope and a pencil and began to write.

It had been the tune that had started it. A Greek tune, called 'Salamis'. It had seemed to Miss Thompson that this was a tune that just had to be sung. She would get the children to sing it. They loved singing, those little ones at the school. And how nice it would be, this tune, sung as a hymn. So while the coach made its way through the Somerset countryside Miss Thompson wrote her hymn.

She wrote two verses. Some 16 lines. These lines expressed how she felt when she read of Jesus saying, 'Suffer the little children to come unto me.' It was a moment in the Gospel story that meant a lot to her. She wanted her little ones in the school to share these feelings and to know that the same Jesus wanted them to come. And so she came to write 'I think when I read that sweet story of old'.

She had always enjoyed writing, had Jemima Thompson. She had always loved hymns. Perhaps she had inherited this from her father, Thomas Thompson of Poundsford Park, famous for his support for all good works. He it was who once offered a prize to whoever could produce 50 hymns suitable for cottage meetings. James Edmeston had won that, Edmeston the great architect, the one who was said to write a new hymn every Sunday afternoon.

Well, Jemima could write too. She had started early with some anonymous contributions to *The Juvenile Magazine*. She had been

13 then. Now she was a young lady and editing another magazine for children. The indefatigable Edmeston was among her contributors. So Jemima wrote her two verses and taught her tune. However she was not quite satisfied. From her earliest days she had wanted to be a missionary. She had been sure, even as a child, that this was to be her calling. She knew that it was to India she would go. Not Africa, not America, not the South Seas, but India.

That was before her illness. After, when she had recovered, they told her she would never go. Not now. That illness had changed everything. However it had not broken her spirit nor dulled her enthusiasm. If she could not go, others could, and she would support them. She would waken the churches and they would send out more missionaries.

So she added a third verse to her hymn:

> But thousands and thousands, who wander and fall,
> Never heard of that heavenly home;
> I should like them to know that there is room for them all,
> And that Jesus has bid them to come.

In 1843, at the age of 30, Jemima married. Samuel Luke was a Congregationalist minister then serving at Clifton. As Mrs Luke Jemima went on writing. She turned out some books that were briefly popular: *The Female Jesuit*, *The Broad Road and the Narrow Way* and others. To the last she eagerly supported the cause of foreign mission and encouraged work among children. In Hope Chapel there is a memorial to Jemima which tells part of the story. The best memorial, however, is her best-known hymn, the one that conveys the great love of her life, the one that she first scribbled on the back of an old envelope while the stage-coach bumped along the road to Wellington.

D

Thomas Goodwin
(1600–1680)

Luke 19:42

Saying, 'Would that even today you knew the things that make for peace! But now they are hid from your eyes.'

We all have our favourite authors. Alexander Whyte had his. In his later years he would often tell students how he had first come under the spell of one particular writer. It had happened back in the 1860s during his own student days in Edinburgh. That was a great time to be a student. Can you imagine it? Novels by both Dickens and Thackeray were appearing in monthly parts, the Brontë sisters were at their very best, Carlyle was at his most influential, George Eliot had just arrived on the scene, and everyone seemed to be reading Ruskin and Macaulay, Tennyson and Browning. Yes, we can well believe that a man might discover a favourite author in those days.

Whyte made his discovery. Yet, while he read all these new writers, and enjoyed them, none of them touched him as did Thomas Goodwin. Sixty years later he was still reading Goodwin. He read him to the last, and Goodwin never failed him.

It has to be said — and Whyte said it himself — Goodwin is not everyone's cup of tea. For Thomas Goodwin was a Puritan and a theologian. He wrote as he had preached, at great length and in great detail. The first volume that Whyte bought consisted of 36 sermons on one chapter of the Bible. Thomas Goodwin was — and is — for those who are prepared to work at their reading.

Wherein, then, lies his power to attract and hold the attention? Goodwin deals with the great questions of life, the great themes of the Bible. He writes not as an academic scholar, but as one who has faced these same questions, and wrestled with these problems, and found in the Scriptures these answers.

Born in the little Norfolk village of Rollesby, Thomas Goodwin went to Cambridge University in 1613. He soon earned a reputation as a scholar, showing marked ability in his studies of Hebrew,

Greek and Latin. That was his problem. Although his parents had hoped that he would become a minister, and had encouraged him to study for that reason, Goodwin rather liked his life at university and enjoyed the success he had earned. It became the great interest of his life to win applause and secure preferment.

At this time his idea of a good preacher was Doctor Senhouse whose flowery style Goodwin thought to cultivate. This, he felt sure, was the way to get on. And getting on was what life was all about.

He was setting out with some of his student friends one day when they heard a bell toll at Christ's College. A funeral service was about to be held, which Goodwin had no thought of attending. However, one of his friends said there would be a sermon and the preacher would be Dr Bambridge. That made Goodwin stop. He had heard of this Bambridge and his reputation for wit and style. This might be worth hearing. So in the two of them went.

The text was from Luke 19:42, the words Jesus spoke as he wept over Jerusalem. The preacher began and Goodwin sat back to enjoy a polished performance. Bambridge spoke with singular directness. He showed that every man has his day, his time when God's grace is freely offered. But that day passes. And if he has not made his peace with God then there can be no more offers. He urged his hearers not to put off their day, but to turn immediately to God.

It was not what Goodwin had expected to hear. It shook him. His friends were waiting for him to rejoin them outside, but instead he went off on his own. 'I thought myself to be as one struck down by a mighty power.' He never forgot that day, an October afternoon in 1620: nothing was ever the same again.

It really did change him. Now he wanted to preach not to win applause but to win souls. His aim in life was no longer to glorify himself but to glorify God. Perhaps it made him less polished in his style, but it gave him the earnestness which made his sermons and books live. It led him, too, into controversy, for there could be no playing safe for such a disciple. This meant a time in exile as well as a full church, but Goodwin was happy to suffer if that would advance the cause of truth.

For Thomas Goodwin the day came. And he found grace. It carried him through a long and busy life and he went quietly home at the end, saying, 'Now I shall be ever with the Lord.'

Henry Francis Lyte
(1793–1847)

Luke 24:29

But they constrained him, saying, 'Stay with us, for it is toward evening and the day is now far spent.' So he went in to stay with them.

Standing on the quay at Brixham in south Devon one is surrounded by memories of great events and famous people. Famous in its day as a fishing port, a pioneer of deep-sea trawling, Brixham is remembered as the place from which the men of Devon sailed to destroy the Spanish Armada. Here, 100 years later, William of Orange landed in the days of the Glorious Revolution. And out there in the bay anchored the ship that was to carry Napoleon to his final exile in St Helena.

Writers and artists have made their home here, people such as Francis Brett Young and Flora Thompson. And here was written one of the most popular and deeply loved of all our hymns. If we listen we will hear the carillon of All Saints Church play it each night at eight o'clock.

Henry Francis Lyte was born in Scotland, at Ednam near Kelso, in 1793. From there the family moved to Ireland and Henry attended school near Enniskillen. Despite their poverty, he was sent to study at Trinity College, Dublin. His first thought had been to follow medicine. However, he felt drawn to the Church and became a curate in 1815, his first post being at Taghmon in County Wexford.

After two years he moved to England to serve as curate at Marazion in Cornwall. One day a neighbouring clergyman sent for Henry. He was dying, this neighbour, and he asked Henry for spiritual guidance. Henry didn't know what to say. But at least he knew where to look. Together they turned to the Bible and discovered there the love of Jesus which is sufficient for all our needs. Words that had once been only words now came alive, and both men were led to a new peace and a deeper joy.

During these years in Cornwall, Henry Lyte paid a visit to Wexford to see an old friend, William Le Hunte, who was ill. They knew he would not recover. All through Henry's visit Le Hunte kept repeating 'abide with me, abide with me'. Of course these words were addressed not to Henry but to Another Friend, and the young curate never forgot the scene, nor did the words fade from his memory.

There followed an unsettled time during which he was 'jostled from one curacy to another'. From Lymington he went to Charlton and from Charlton to Dittisham. This time he found very wearing. And doubtless he was cheered when in 1823 he learned that he was to be appointed to Lower Brixham where he was to be the first incumbent.

Lyte stayed in Brixham for 23 years, living first in Burton Street and later at Berry Head House. These were not easy years. Quite simply the locals did not at first understand their new minister. They could not appreciate his rare qualities and tender spirit. They themselves were a hardy lot, sailors and fishermen, living a rough and often dangerous life. He was not the kind of man to establish an immediate rapport with folk like this.

So his work in Brixham was difficult. Henry Lyte was often hurt and disappointed, but he refused to give in. Gradually things began to change. As is often the case, success first came with the children. Eventually Lyte had a Sunday School of some 800 children for which he trained a staff of 70 teachers. Through the children he found a way to reach the parents. Slowly the whole community came to be affected by his influence. Visitors, too, were contacted. It is said that every ship that came into the port was given a Bible by the minister.

But the strain of these years was great and Henry had never been strong. By 1847 he was a sick man. His only hope of recovery, he was told, was to leave at once for the warmer climate of southern Europe. His family convinced him that he should go. The arrangements were made and he preached his farewell sermon on 5 September. After the service, as he sat resting at Berry Head House, looking out over Tor Bay, he wrote a poem. He had always liked writing poetry; at university he had gained a number of prizes with his verses and had since published a number of books.

As he sat there, knowing that his time was short, and that the move to Nice was only postponing the inevitable, his mind went back to the days at Wexford and the words that his friend had repeated so earnestly as a prayer. Henry knew that the words owed their inspiration to Luke's story of the walk to Emmaus and the disciples' request to Jesus: 'Stay with us for it is toward evening and the day is now far spent.' Now, in the evening of his own life, with his own day already far spent, Henry found a particular comfort in this passage. And once more he asked Jesus 'to abide with me'. There was neither fear nor gloom in his heart. And there is none in his poem. Its notes are quiet confidence and calm trust. This is his 'legacy to his family and the world'.

Henry Armstrong
(1912–   )

John 1:6–14

There was a man sent from God, whose name was John. [7]He came for testimony, to bear witness to the light, that all might believe through him. [8]He was not the light, but came to bear witness to the light.

[9]The true light that enlightens every man was coming into the world. [10]He was in the world, and the world was made through him, yet the world knew him not. [11]He came to his own home, and his own people received him not. [12]But to all who received him, who believed in his name, he gave power to become children of God: [13]who were born, not of blood nor of the will of the flesh nor of the will of man, but of God.

[14]And the Word became flesh and dwelt among us, full of grace and truth; we have beheld his glory, glory as of the only Son from the Father.

'Henry Armstrong, what are you doing there?' Judge Ida May Adams stared at the man standing before her. He was one of the drunks lifted by the city police the previous night. He had crashed his car into a lamp post out by 18th Street. When arrested he had struggled. He looked sick and tired and nothing like a man who only nine years earlier had been champion of the whole world.

'Henry,' the judge's voice was quiet, 'you're letting down a million boys.' He scarcely heard the rest of it, the suspended sentence, the words of advice; these words had shaken him. 'Letting down a million boys . . .'

He had always wanted to be a hero. Even when he was just Henry Jackson, another poor boy from Columbus, Mississippi. Things had been tough then and they had got little better when the family moved to Missouri in search of work. Things got a whole lot worse when his mother died and his father took to drink. Henry left school and got a job as a labourer on the railway.

Then one day he read something in a newspaper that made him

think. He read how Kid Chocolate, a negro from Cuba, had just received 75 000 dollars for one fight in New York. That was it. Henry would be a boxer. One day he too would have his name in the papers and take home 75 000 dollars.

And that day came. It was rather slow in coming. The first few years had been terrible: fights were few and purses were small, and Henry had lived as a tramp, hiding on board freight trains, hitching lifts, begging for food. He refused to give up his dream. After some time he got the 'right' manager, the kind a coloured boy had to have if he was to get anywhere. And he began to attract a following.

'Little Doc Destruction' they called him, 'Homicide Hank', 'Hammering Henry'. His fighting style of non-stop aggression soon produced results, startling results. In 1937 he won his first title. The following year he won a second world championship and some months later he took a third. It had never happened before; no man had ever held three world titles at the same time. It was unbelievable. But it was true. Henry Armstrong had gained a unique place in the history of his sport. He was famous, and very rich. His dream had come true.

The strange thing was that while enjoying his money and his success, Henry felt that something was still missing. He had got what he wanted but somehow it did not make him happy in the way he had thought it would.

Of course it could not last. The titles, won so dearly and worn so proudly, were lost. The last defeat, the one for the welterweight championship, was the worst. He had been so confident before the fight, the first rounds had gone so well, but by the end he was beaten, badly beaten, and he knew that he was no longer the tireless athlete of old. The great days had gone.

He fought on. Mostly he won but some he lost and they were the big ones. Lost too was most of the money, maybe as much as a million dollars. He wasn't even sure. So Henry chased the good times with increasing frenzy. That solved nothing. He started to drink heavily. And found himself in court before Judge Adams.

Her words hurt him. He later said she hurt him more than any fighter ever did. So, once released, he went out to drown his self-pity. He did it too. He wasn't feeling any pain when he got behind the wheel to drive home. He was on the Malibu road, hitting 75 miles an hour when he blacked out. He came to still at the wheel and the car still on the road.

He pulled over. And as he sat there wondering at his escape a hand hit him in the face. He felt it but as he looked around there was no one there! Suddenly he saw it all, the utter futility of his life, the need for a new start before it really was too late. He drove slowly home.

In the bedroom he picked up his Bible. He turned the pages. His eye was caught by these verses in John. They seemed to refer to him: he had refused Jesus a place in his life. He read on. Power! Power enough to rebuild his life, to start again? And there on his knees Henry Armstrong handed over his life to Christ.

Word soon went round that something had happened to Henry Armstrong. Some folk laughed. Most wondered how long it would last. But one man went over to see him. He was a local minister and he went to ask Henry to preach for him. He refused. Later, perhaps... 'No,' said the minister, 'it's happened to you. Tell folk about it. That's your sermon.'

Henry Armstrong did go and tell the folk. He went on to become an ordained minister. He also began working with boys, the boys he had once let down. Now he had something to tell them, a power to share with them. He would not let them down again.

Samuel Johnson, Walter Scott, R M McCheyne
(1709–1784)   (1771–1832)   (1813–1843)

John 9:4

We must work the works of him who sent me, while it is day; night comes, when no one can work.

Dr Samuel Johnson. Sir Walter Scott. Robert Murray McCheyne. What do they have in common? Well, the first two are easy: Johnson and Scott are of course famous writers, two of the giants of literature. And that's not all. Each of them is the subject of a well-known biography: Boswell's *Life of Johnson* and Lockhart's *Life of Scott*. Classics. But what about the third man? What about this McCheyne? Who was he? What did he do?

Robert Murray McCheyne was a minister. In Dundee. For seven years. He wasn't quite 30 when he died. Yet that young man, in those seven short years, left a mark on the city of Dundee and on the people of Scotland. There was a rare power to his preaching, a power that changed lives. And he has never been forgotten. Yes, but that still doesn't answer the question: what does he have in common with Johnson and Scott?

Is it the fact that he, too, had his biography written? That book, written by his friend Andrew Bonar, is itself something of a classic: *Memoir and Remains of R M McCheyne*. So is that the answer?

No. For these three men have something else in common. It is a motto, a motto that each chose for himself. Johnson had it engraved on his watch. Scott had it carved on his sundial. McCheyne used it as his personal seal. A motto. Just two words, two Greek words — ερXεται νυξ — 'night is coming'.

It's taken from this passage in John 9. Each of these three men took that message to heart. 'Night comes', so do it now! That work that is yours, do it now. That good deed, don't hesitate, do it now. That kind word, don't wait, say it now. While you can. Don't wait until you feel like it. Don't wait until you're in the mood.

That's what happens, isn't it? We put it off; we'll do it later, we say, when we've more time, when we feel more like it. We'll do it then. Only, sometimes it never gets done.

There are many things we were going to do with our lives. When we got the time. People we meant to see. Letters we meant to write. Phone calls we were going to return. For some of these things it is already too late. We could have done it. We meant to do it. But we put it off. And we can't do it now.

That's what a lot of people do with Jesus. Sure, they say, I'll think about it. But not right now. I'm up to my ears at the moment. Can't you see how busy I am? Yes, they mean to come to church. One day they will sit down and read their Bibles. Yes, they really must think about God and Jesus, and they will. But not right now. Do it now, says Jesus. 'Night comes.'

Now the thing about Johnson, Scott and McCheyne is this, they were all very busy men, they packed their days with activity. They got so much done, each of them, that we might be tempted to think they were just lucky, lucky to be born with abnormal energy and an excess of leisure. Not at all. They were not so very different either in temperament or in circumstance. But this was different — they realised how easy it is to waste time and they resolved to do something about it. McCheyne once said, 'What right have I to steal and abuse my Master's time?'

And this is what they each did; they turned to Jesus and took his words seriously. That's always the right place to start. They took these particular words, in the Greek, and put them where they could always see them. They didn't say, 'how wise of Jesus', and then forget all about it. No, they wrote down that message and kept it where it would be seen. And it worked because they took it to heart.

There are things to be done. Little things, big things. There is work for us all, something that we can do to make the world a better place. So — let's get on with it. Quietly, calmly, gladly, let's do what we can today.

> Give to each flying minute
> Something to keep in store
> Work, for the night is coming
> When man works no more.

Agatha Christie
(1891–1976)

John 10:11

I am the good shepherd. The good shepherd lays down his life for the sheep.

The little church at Churston Ferrers was, she felt, very beautiful. There was only one thing: the east window had plain glass. That was wrong. It looked as odd as a missing tooth. And how lovely it would look, that same window, in colours, especially pale colours.

So something should be done. And she would do it. She would give the necessary money. She would write a story and, from the proceeds, she would pay for a stained-glass window. It would, she decided, be a simple window and a happy window, with clear pictures that children could enjoy. She looked around for an artist.

That proved to be more difficult than she had imagined. However, in the end she found a studio in Bideford and a man called Patterson who used colour in a way she liked. Then the real problem surfaced. As it was an east window, both the artist and the Diocese of Exeter told her that the central pattern had to be the crucifixion. She wanted a picture of the good shepherd. To her this was very important. She wanted children to look at this window and to be made happy by it. What better way to show Jesus, she argued, than as the good shepherd?

The experts gave in. They excused themselves by saying that the shepherd would, after all, be quite fitting in a pastoral parish. Perhaps that was their genuine conviction. At any rate, the shepherd with his lamb was chosen. Other simple Gospel scenes were incorporated in the design. And in the end everyone seems to have been happy.

That decision — to show Jesus as the good shepherd — was very much in keeping with her attitude to children. Nor was there anything incongruous in the First Lady of Crime worrying about church windows. There is further 'evidence' of her deep interest in bringing the Gospel to children in her *Star over Bethlehem*, a collection of stories and poems written for young folk.

Her own childhood as Agatha Miller had been spent in Torquay. It had been, she always said, a very happy childhood. A very happy part of it had been going to church. She also found very great pleasure in the stories of the Bible. They were, she insisted, from a child's viewpoint 'rattling good yarns'. Church and Bible were to play a meaningful part all through her life. So, too, it turned out, were 'rattling good yarns'.

It was as Agatha Christie, working during the First World War as a VAD nurse in a dispensary, that she first thought of writing a detective story. Prompted by a bet made with her sister Madge, she started to write. In 1920 *The Mysterious Affair at Styles* was published by John Lane of Bodley Head. A copy of that original edition, complete with dust cover, would now fetch in excess of £3500.

The explanation for this startlingly high price is simple: Agatha Christie went on to write some 80 books and become one of the most popular writers in history with world sales topping the three million mark. So her first book, the one that started it all, is of unusual interest to collectors.

Her success was not instantaneous. Six publishers turned down that first book, and it was not until her seventh book — *The Murder of Roger Ackroyd* — that her sales began to climb. That success was due in part to her 'disappearance' in 1926 when massive police and press searches brought her name to a wider public. It also left her with an understandable dislike of publicity.

The simple fact was that she went through a bad time then — how bad she would never say — and she suffered a breakdown. Perhaps the choice of Jesus as good shepherd had a special significance for one who had experienced the misery of being 'lost'.

A very private person, especially in her later years, Agatha Christie led a peaceful life, delighting in her family and thriving on her work. In her own way, quietly and without fuss, she liked to give happiness to others. In an obvious sense she did this with her books and her plays. She did it in other ways too.

From the profits from her writing she gave to various projects. Westminster Abbey is known to have benefited. However the gift to Churston Ferrers was a particularly happy one. It enabled her to employ her special skills for the sake of others. She could have simply given the money and in a way that would have been using her talents to help. This way, however, undertaking a piece of work expressly for the purpose of paying for the window, made it much more personal. Doing it left her feeling 'both proud and humble'. Using our talents for others brings its own reward.

James McCosh
(1811–1894)

John 16:7–16

Nevertheless I tell you the truth: it is to your advantage that I go away, for if I do not go away, the Counsellor will not come to you; but if I go, I will send him to you. [8]And when he comes, he will convince the world of sin and of righteousness and of judgment: [9]of sin, because they do not believe in me; [10]of righteousness, because I go to the Father, and you will see me no more; [11]of judgment, because the ruler of this world is judged.

[12]'I have yet many things to say to you, but you cannot bear them now. [13]When the Spirit of truth comes, he will guide you into all the truth; for he will not speak on his own authority, but whatever he hears he will speak, and he will declare to you the things that are to come. [14]He will glorify me, for he will take what is mine and declare it to you. [15]All that the Father has is mine; therefore I said that he will take what is mine and declare it to you.

[16]'A little while, and you will see me no more; again a little while, and you will see me.'

The service would begin in a few minutes and the visiting preacher was almost ready to enter the church when there was a knock at the vestry door. He looked up expecting to see the beadle or one of the elders. He saw a stranger. Yet even before the man spoke he knew who he was. Everyone knew that Dr McCosh was home from America on a visit to his sister. The Dr McCosh, the President of Princeton College, the famous philosopher. He had come, he said, with a request. He wondered if the preacher would be so kind as to allow him to preach? It would be the last chance he would ever have to speak in the church of his boyhood.

James McCosh was born in 1811 at the farm of Carskeoch in the Ayrshire parish of Straiton. His father had been a relatively prosperous farmer with a genuine interest in theology and an intense loyalty to his local church. Every Sunday they would walk the five miles to the church. Not that McCosh retained the happiest memories of those Sundays. He later remarked that he had never heard one word of Gospel truth.

What was lacking in Sunday worship was made up for at home. McCosh's memories of family worship were much happier. It came as no great surprise when he told his mother that he felt called to the ministry. Off he went to complete his studies at Glasgow and Edinburgh. McCosh was not the poorest student of his time but conditions, especially in Glasgow, were less than comfortable. McCosh remembered this. It was to be important.

However, he enjoyed his student days, worked hard, gained prizes, and discovered an enthusiasm for philosophy. He also came under the spell of Thomas Chalmers. All of which was also to have important repercussions.

McCosh became minister at Brechin. He described the old cathedral city as 'a noisy street with dull grey houses'. Yet he was happy there and got involved in many educational and welfare schemes. He also married the daughter of the local doctor. It seemed he was there to stay.

Then came the storm. McCosh was present at the Disruption Assembly, walked out, signed the deed (he's there quite prominently in Hill's picture), and came home to start again. He took most of the congregation with him, and after meeting for a time in the granary of the local distillery, they built a new church in Brechin. It still seemed as if McCosh would stay.

Two other things happened about this time. First of all, he became responsible for supplying the new Free Church gatherings in his area. So he was forced to travel, and we find him riding up to 30 miles a day, conducting services in fields and by the roadside. That was itself a new experience and rather unsettling. Then he wrote a book. On philosophy. He launched it with some misgivings. *The Method of Divine Government* made him famous, and it changed his life completely.

One of those who read the book was the Earl of Clarendon. He decided that here was the man for the chair of philosophy at the new Queen's College of Belfast. There was considerable controversy over this appointment, the Ulster folk feeling, not unreasonably, that they could find their own professors. Thackeray wrote some humourous lines on 'the insult that's done to this nation' with the appointment of 'the Saxon McCosh'. McCosh was surprised himself, but accepted.

McCosh was happy in Belfast. He published more books and,

while serving as an elder in a city congregation, also went out preaching. He was a first-hand witness of the famous '59 Revival and wrote an interesting account of what he saw. Although he made frequent visits to Scotland to visit his mother, he declined the chair offered by the Free Church in their new college in Glasgow. He did, however, leave Belfast.

In 1868 McCosh was invited to become President of Princeton. He was a distinguished figure in academic circles, although it must be said he was not an original thinker. It was whispered at the time that he was a compromise candidate, brought in to heal divisions and hopefully to restore the rather fading fortunes of Princeton.

McCosh made a wise president. He taught and had considerable influence on his students. He was good with students, being mindful of his own college days, and anxious to help the poorer among them. His wife also took an interest in the students. She also kept Dr McCosh from ever getting too important. When he once claimed of a portrait that it made him look as if he had no teeth, she replied, 'James, you have none. It's a fine picture.'

McCosh did much to build up the college. He introduced new ideas, secured a gymnasium, and a hospital. He was good at finding benefactors such as John Green who had made a fortune in the China trade. He was also good at recruiting students. To some he was too strict and he did have his critics among the staff, but he was popular with most, who held him in reverent affection, and referred to him in later years as 'old Jimmy'.

This, then, was the man in the vestry, asking to preach. Of course the preacher agreed. He was interested himself to hear the famous philosopher. McCosh preached from John 16. Speaking, as he said, for the last time in his old church, he dwelt on the promise of Jesus to his disciples that when he left them the Comforter would come. In that same promise the old professor rested his hope. The Comforter had been with him through a long life and he could now leave his old home and his family there, knowing that the Spirit of peace and love would be with them and with him.

Thomas Burns
(1796–1871)

Acts 1:8

> But you shall receive power when the Holy Spirit has come upon you; and you shall be my witness in Jerusalem and in all Judea and Samar'ia and to the end of the earth.

It was just the word Thomas Burns wanted to hear. It was the word he himself would have given. They were gathered there in Free St George's, Edinburgh, the pilgrims and their friends, those who would shortly sail and those who would stay behind. It was important that the right note be struck. There would be 237 souls leaving on the *Philip Laing*. They would be travelling across the oceans to a new life in New Zealand. They must be sent off not only with good wishes but with something more. And that something more John Sym gave them as he preached to his text.

Emigrating was something that Thomas Burns felt he had to do. There was a new world to be built and he believed he was called to help in its building. He had been thinking of going to New Zealand for the past ten years and more. Now the time had come.

Thomas Burns was Robert Burns' nephew. He had been born at Mossgiel in 1796. After student days at Edinburgh, he had been the parish minister at Ballantrae. From there he came to the parish of Monkton and Prestwick in 1830. Here he showed those qualities of leadership that were to be so important later. In particular he was largely responsible for the building of a new church, a large and beautiful building of which he was not a little proud.

Burns was also proud of his garden and glebe. It was said that he kept seven cows, 'and sold the milk'. The garden was famous all over the county. And, for that matter, the stipend was considerable. All of which is important. There came the day when, for conscience sake, Thomas Burns walked out of his comfortable manse and left the church he had built. He was there at the

114

Disruption Assembly (1843) and walked out with his colleagues from Newton-on-Ayr and Barr. It did not make things easier that he left the manse at the time when his garden was at its loveliest. Nor did it help when his wife was injured lifting some heavy furniture. But he never hesitated.

The family found accommodation in an old public house near Prestwick Toll. There Burns set to work building up a new congregation. Most of his people came with him and, after worshipping for some months in the open air — with a never-to-be-forgotten communion service held during a downpour — Burns' energetic leadership resulted in a church being built in the village of Monkton. Not that Burns stayed at home. He helped other Free Church congregations find their feet and for a time he was in charge of the congregation at Portobello. This was the best possible experience for his colonial adventure.

There is no doubt that it was Thomas Burns who turned a dream into reality. He it was who travelled the country, winning support and finding settlers. He made it happen. And, when they did sail, although Captain Ellis was in command, Burns was the real leader. He was a tower of strength during the long voyage, 139 days at sea. He saw that the settlers fitted into a busy daily round of services and classes. Burns himself taught two groups of young men and women, and he organised others into finding work.

He took the services himself, two every day with full traditional services on the Sunday. During bad weather his was a calming influence. Personally he rather seemed to enjoy the storms but he was an expert at stilling fear among the more nervous.

He quietened other fears too. When they finally anchored off the Otago coast the settlers were dismayed to see the high hills that came down to the water's edge. They started to grumble. How could they possibly work such steep ground? And would you look at the great forests with those gigantic trees! And what about those fierce natives, and what had the pilot meant when he said they were looking out for the fattest settlers?

It was Burns who spoke up. He got everyone on deck, explained that they would be settling in the plains beyond the hills and suggested that those big trees only proved what a fertile place it was. The natives, he added, were friendly.

Of course it was rough at first. They had to build their own houses, and they had to sleep out until they had built them. But build them they did. The city of Dunedin has grown from these humble beginnings.

Thomas Burns lived to see his dream come true. He lived to be respected and honoured. To the last he remembered why they had left Scotland and that text from Acts remained his inspiration.

Lady Nairne
(1766–1845)

Romans 8:32
He who did not spare his own Son but gave him up for us all, will he not also give us all things with him?

Driving through the village one day the major's wife noticed that a crowd had gathered. She stopped to see what was happening. Someone, it became clear, was selling something. Whatever it was he seemed to have plenty of customers. She was more curious than ever and sent to find out. To her surprise, she discovered that a traveller was selling ballads. She bought one of his books, only to find the songs were quite indecent. She went home saddened to think that the folk had nothing better to sing. Couldn't someone do something about it?

Couldn't she? Why not indeed? The thought came to her that she herself:

> For puir auld Scotland's sake
> Some usefu' plan or beuk could make
> Or sing a song at least.

The songs began to appear in *The Scottish Minstrel*. From the first they were eagerly received. Some, it is true, were based on older songs, but all of them had an unmistakable character. Some were sentimentally Jacobite, full of a sad longing for the Bonnie Prince. Others were alive with humour. Wed to beautiful tunes, they quickly found a place in Scottish hearts. It has been argued that only Robert Burns gave the people more songs. There was, however, a question about these songs.

As they continued to appear in the *Minstrel* — songs such as 'The Land o' the Leal', 'Caller Herrin', 'The Laird o' Cockpen', 'The Rowan Tree', 'The Auld Hoose', 'The Hundred Pipers' and the others — people wondered as to the identity of the writer. The songs carried only a set of initials: 'BB'. Who, everyone asked, was this BB?

117

People had been arguing over 'the Great Unknown' who was producing the *Waverley* novels. Here was a second puzzle to intrigue and annoy. A little light was shed on the mystery when it was revealed that the initials 'BB' stood for 'Mrs Bogan of Bogan'. But who was she? No one could tell, and no one would say.

In the meantime the major's wife had become Lady Nairne. Her husband's title was restored by reversal of attainder, the family's old Jacobite sympathies no longer being held against them. As Lady Nairne she was a familiar figure in Edinburgh. Then, on her husband's death in 1830, she went first to Ireland and then to the continent before returning to live at Gask in Perthshire.

There she had been born as Carolina Oliphant in the 'auld hoose' of her song. That house was gone, pulled down some 40 years before her return. But there was a new house and there were the old memories. Memories of the old laird, her father, and memories of her mother who died when Carolina was eight. The mother's last words had been, 'See which of you will be the best bairn,' and then, turning to her husband, she said, 'You see how easily I can part with my bairns, for I know they are in good hands.'

Little Carolina Oliphant knew those good hands and at an early age learned to trust them. She had, she later wrote, a favourite verse that spoke to her of God's love. How could she doubt the love of a God who 'did not spare his own Son'? All through her life, as a shy little girl learning to dance, as a lovely young lady admired as the Flower of Strathearn, as the major's wife, as a baron's widow, through all the years her faith was fresh and strong.

She kept the secret of her authorship to the end. There were 87 songs all told, most of them still sung today. It was only after her death in 1845 that a collection of her songs appeared as *Lays from Strathearn*. For the first time her name was published.

There was another secret she kept to the end. She had sold all the family plate and given the money to her church. Always generous, she had been anxious to do something in a time of crisis. As with her songs, this was a gift for which she sought neither thanks nor reward. After all, what was all her giving when her Father 'did not spare his own Son'?

Robert Bruce
(1554–1631)

Romans 8:38–9
For I am sure that neither death, nor life, nor angels, nor principalities, nor things present, nor things to come, nor powers, [39]nor height, nor depth, nor anything else in all creation, will be able to separate us from the love of God in Christ Jesus our Lord.

The old Stirlingshire town of Larbert does not attract many tourists. Nor, at first sight, is there anything noteworthy about the parish church. And even if you were dragged round the graveyard and shown one particular stone you would still wonder why we'd stopped here. For there is nothing remarkable about this stone. It is obviously old and it is, equally obviously, badly cracked. It carries a faded coat of arms, a Latin inscription, a date and a set of initials. All this fails to make it one of the most beautiful stones in Scotland, and falls far short of making it one of the most interesting.

Yet there is a story here. And some patient detective work will uncover more than we might imagine.

For a start, that coat of arms tells us something. The person buried here must have belonged to some noble family. Right. Then perhaps the inscription is a family motto? It is in fact taken from the Bible and translates into the familiar text 'Christ in life or death is gain'. This suggests that the inscription is after all more personal than a family motto. It suggests that this man — or woman — was known for leading a religious life.

The date is 1631, the year of this person's death. So, putting it together, we have a religious person, belonging to a noble family, connected some way to Larbert, who died in 1631. And we've got the initials. There's M — I'll give you that — it stands for Master. Then there's R and B. Master RB. Master Robert Bruce, Laird of Kinnaird and minister of the Gospel.

Robert Bruce. It sounds familiar. It should, for he is a descendant of King Robert the Bruce. There is royal blood in his veins. His father Alexander Bruce of Aird Castle is a baron of the old school, wealthy and powerful, with ambitions for his sons. Robert is the second son and, being an able lad, the baron decides to send him off to study Law and become a Lord of Session.

So off Robert goes to St Andrew's University at the age of 14. Unfortunately for family ambition, young Robert comes under the influence of old John Knox. And that starts something. At first, however, all is well. Having taken his degree, Master Robert Bruce is packed off to France for further study. He comes home after his years there and takes up his legal career. So far all is going to plan.

But, unknown to his family, Robert is all this while fighting a battle. A quiet, personal, painful battle. He himself is happy with the future mapped out for him, but there's this voice inside that keeps telling him that God has another plan for him, a very different plan. Robert feels that God wants him to be a minister. He has fought against this conviction, he has tried to ignore it, but on the night of 31 August 1581 God wrestles for his soul. The next morning Robert gets up and tells the family that he is going back to St Andrew's to study for the ministry. They don't like it. He knew they wouldn't. But he knows now that this is the road he must take.

It proves to be a very strange road. It leads him to the pulpit of St Giles in Edinburgh. It takes him twice to the Moderator's chair in the Assembly. It takes him into the esteem and under the patronage of the king. This road even leads him to act as a Privy Councillor, and for a brief time in 1590 to be King James' most trusted adviser. A road to fame! Here is James saying that Bruce is worth half his kingdom. And here, at the same time, are the people, the ordinary people who crowd the church to listen to him preach. While here are the young ministers of the church, the best of them, coming to seek his advice and guidance. Yes, Robert Bruce is doing rather well. His is a pleasant life of ability recognised and virtue honoured.

Until, that is, he is asked to act as spokesman for the Church, against the king. A wise man would find an excuse, but Bruce is never wise as the world counts wisdom. He goes to the king, he speaks up, and he falls from favour. Just at this point there is the strange event known to history as the Gowrie Incident. The king issues his own version of the affair and orders all ministers to read this from their pulpits. Bruce refuses. It's not so much that he doubts the king — he is inclined to believe him — rather it's that he believes the king has no right to order ministers to read any such thing from their pulpits. He knows what will happen. Bruce is sent into exile, and when he is allowed back he is sent to Inverness to be out of the road.

Eventually he was permitted to return to Kinnaird. While there he rebuilds Larbert Church and ministers to the people who still crowd to hear him. The end came in 1631.

Yes, Robert Bruce once had everything. And he gave it all up to stay true to his Master. It would have been easy to pretend, to find the words to justify staying quiet, to have played the king's game and kept all that went with it. But for Robert Bruce there was no question about what to do.

That last morning at Kinnaird he came down to breakfast. He told his family that he would sup that same night with his Master. The last thing he did was to ask his daughter to take the Bible and read from Romans 8, the last two verses. And here, in this great promise of Christ's unchanging love, Robert Bruce went to rest.

Sir William Dobbie
(1879–1964)

Romans 15:4

For whatever was written in former days was written for our instruction, that by steadfastness and by the encouragement of the scriptures we might have hope.

The letter is signed George RI. And it goes like this, 'To honour her brave people I award the George Cross to the Island Fortress of Malta to bear witness to a heroism and devotion that will long be famous in history.'

That letter was sent in April 1942 to the Governor of Malta, Lieutenant General Sir William Dobbie. Churchill described him as 'that extraordinary man — the heroic defender of Malta'. Dobbie was actually retired when the war broke out, but he offered himself for service and in 1940 he was sent to Malta as governor. He had had a long career in the army. He fought in France during the First World War, where he was decorated and promoted. He subsequently served in Egypt, Palestine and Malaya as well as putting in time in the War Office.

All of which may seem a strange life for a Christian. Dobbie was a Christian, an earnest, praying, Bible-reading Christian. He had been born in India and was a schoolboy on holiday in England when, in his own words, 'I accepted Jesus Christ as my Saviour.' He was then 14. The change was real and lasting. He himself had no difficulty in reconciling his faith with his military career. In fact he once wrote a pamphlet on the subject, concluding from his study of the Bible that it is both 'honourable' and 'well fitting' for a Christian to serve as a soldier.

This, then, was the man sent to Malta. Sent to do the seemingly impossible, to hold the island against the combined forces of Italy and Germany. Malta was certainly a very important base and it had to be held. But it was a lonely outpost in those dark days, 1000 miles from the nearest friend and surrounded by enemies. Its resources were totally inadequate. The garrison was small and ill-equipped. Supplies and reinforcements could come in only by sea. When Dobbie arrived there were only four aircraft on the island, the four Gloster Gladiators that had been discovered in crates in the dockyard stores. There were only 16 anti-aircraft guns on the whole island. Add to this the fact of a large civilian population who could not be evacuated and who would have to be fed. Open to invasion, to bombing, and to the danger of starvation, the situation was grim. Someone said that only a miracle could save Malta. Dobbie prayed for the miracle.

His first Order of the Day was very much to the point. He told the garrison, 'it may be that hard times lie ahead of us, but however hard they may be, I know that the courage and determination of all ranks will not falter and that with God's help we will maintain the security of this fortress.' In that spirit they faced the attack. During the next two years there were some 2000 air raids on Malta. There was an attack by the Italian navy on Valletta. Supply convoys were constantly harried from the sea and from the air. Much damage was done and heavy casualties suffered. But Malta survived.

Dobbie's part in this was of the first importance. During the worst of the raids he could be found up on the roof watching. He was here with the troops and there with the people, and everywhere his was a calming presence. His broadcasts built up morale and his prayer meetings in the Governor's Palace meant much to all who attended.

He made no secret of his faith. Rather he willingly pointed others to the source. For him the Bible was all important in those years. Romans 15:4 was a key passage: God was inviting him to turn to the Bible to find there in its pages a message for his own situation. Later he said, 'We were faced with many and great difficulties ... but I found we were not the first to be so situated ... these records have been deliberately placed there for our learning so that we might have comfort and peace.' In particular Dobbie saw in the Bible how people, 'When they asked for God's help and asked in faith, he gave it to them and delivered them.'

It worked. Passage after passage seemed to speak to their situation: 'This was true for them,' he wrote, 'it was also true for us.' The story in 2 Kings 6, the servant's feat and Elisha's answer — 'those who are with us are more than those who are with them' — brought much encouragement. So too the story of Hezekiah during the siege of Jerusalem. And King Jehoshaphat, under attack from the Ammonites and Moabites, receiving the promise, 'Be not afraid for the battle is not yours but God's.' All these, said Dobbie, 'so exactly fitted our case ... that they might have been written expressly for us'.

There was another lesson from this Bible reading. And it was summed up in Nehemiah's word, 'We prayed to God and set a watch.' While putting his trust in God and seeing God's hand at work during the seige, Dobbie knew that he and his men had their part to play. He knew they had to do their duty faithfully. 'We did all we could possibly think,' he said, adding, 'but our reliance was on God.' True Christianity does not make men irresponsible or unrealistic. But it gives them something more. Dobbie learned this from the Bible and saw its truth in the siege of Malta.

The Earl of Shaftesbury
(1801–1885)

1 Corinthians 4:7

For who sees anything different in you? What have you that you did not receive? If then you received it, why do you boast as if it were not a gift?

In Piccadilly Circus, at the centre of London's West End, stands one of the most famous statues in the world: that winged archer we call Eros. He appeared there in 1893, the work of Sir Alfred Gilbert. And it caused a major row, a row that cost Sir Alfred his membership of the Royal Academy. For, you see, that statue, paid for by public subscription, was a memorial to a very famous and much-loved man. People thought that such a statue should at least look like the man it commemorated. Especially when the man was Anthony Ashley-Cooper, the seventh Earl of Shaftesbury.

The seventh earl was rather special. For more than 50 years he waged a war, a war fought on many fronts, against many enemies, yet a war with one clear objective: to help those who couldn't help themselves.

As a young MP, elected in 1826, he first took up the cudgels for a very sad and neglected group, those known officially as 'pauper lunatics'. They were then just locked out of sight and forgotten. Shaftesbury was the first to do something to change things. He pushed two bills through parliament, giving lunatics recognition and protection. Nor did he stop there. For the rest of his life he kept on working for them as Chairman of the Lunacy Commission.

That was just the start. There were other victims of the new society produced by the Industrial Revolution. There were the women and the children of the mills, with their 12-hour day and appalling conditions. 'Dark satanic mills' indeed. It took Shaftesbury 14 years to get a ten-hour day passed by parliament. Then there were the chimney sweeps, the boys who climbed the chimneys. Shaftesbury took up their cause and helped end that murderous trade. There were the women and children slaving in the mines, dragging coal tubs underground. He fought for them and won their freedom. There were the agricultural labourers. He worked for them. The victims of the Irish famine. He mobilised support. And on he went.

Although he was a happily married family man, Shaftesbury had no time for hobbies or amusements. He took up every good cause. Eventually he was involved with some 200 organisations, writing, speaking, visiting on their behalf. It never stopped. Shaftesbury was 84 when he died and hard at work to the last.

'The Poor Man's Earl' they called him, 'the Father of Reform'. A monument in Westminster Abbey talks of his 'long life spent in the cause of the helpless and the suffering'. Gladstone said his name would be 'ever gratefully remembered'.

And what made him like that? Why did he care when others didn't bother? And why did he work so very hard at it? Well, he tells us himself. Shaftesbury wanted to be buried in the family vault at Winborne in Dorsetshire. He wanted three texts for the memorial tablet in the church. The first one was this: 1 Corinthians 4:7. It was Shaftesbury's conviction that our lives are given us to be used in the Master's work, in helping his children. Whatever we have has been given to us to be used. Our wealth, if we have any; our talents, few or many; our time, long or short; all have been given to us for a purpose. And that purpose is to do good. Shaftesbury's one fear was that he wasn't doing enough. A Christian, he believed, knowing the love of Jesus, can never do too much. He will always see something else that needs to be done. And when he sees it he will do it.

Today there are still some 37 organisations, religious and benevolent, that carry on work begun by Shaftesbury. Of course times have changed. Many of the battles he fought have been won. There is now a welfare state where, in theory at least, all are cared for, from cradle to grave. Yet the war itself is not over, there are still wrongs to be put right, still people to be helped. Our own modern society, 100 and more years after Shaftesbury's death, our enlightened, caring society, has victims of its own. There are new problems. The poor are always with us.

Which means, of course, that there is work to be done. Just as in his day. So in our own. And there are difficulties along the way.

Just as there were then. And there is still the same reason for getting involved. What we have has been given to us to be used. Every talent. For the Master.

So as we face the challenge of our situation we go forward remembering the motto of Shaftesbury: 'Love — serve'. That will carry us on.

The Duchess of Gordon
(1794–1865)

1 Corinthians 7:20
Every one should remain in the state in which he was called.

The Duchess of Gordon had a problem. With the death of her husband, George, the fifth Duke, she had the opportunity to retire from public life. This was what she wanted to do. On the other hand, by retaining her place in society it was possible that she could use her position to do good. It was a difficult choice and the duchess was perhaps not entirely sure as to her own motives.

However, she knew where to turn for guidance. She laid the matter before God in prayer, and she found her answer in the Bible, in the First Letter to the Church at Corinth. There, in the seventh chapter, felt the duchess, was God's word to her: she was to continue as duchess.

Elizabeth Brodie had been a duchess for something less than nine years. She had married her husband when he was the Marquis of Huntly. It had been a happy marriage, although there had been no children. They had had a pleasant enough time at Huntly Lodge and Gordon Castle. But a visit to another stately home had rather changed things.

They went to stay with the Duke of Manchester at Kimbolton Castle. While there Elizabeth experienced a religious awakening. It was not altogether unexpected, for she had been thinking seriously about her life ever since a visit to London had revealed one rather shocking example of vice in high places. That incident had been the start of the process that came to a head at Kimbolton. The change was to have far-reaching results.

Having come to her decision the duchess looked for ways to use her position. She began with monthly conferences for ministers. These were held at Huntly Lodge, the ministers being invited as her guests. The conferences would then finish with public services in the church. This led her to initiate local missionary activity. Men such as Duncan Matheson were employed to preach in areas seldom visited by the parish ministers. Large crowds were reached at the half-yearly feeing markets, and the smallest clachan was not neglected.

One evangelist whose activities the duchess always warmly supported was Brownlow North. She had known him in his earlier days, the days when this young aristocrat was fast building himself an evil reputation. In fact she had helped him towards his new life. Thereafter she gave him every encouragement and had copies of his pamphlet *Six Short Rules for Young Christians* sent to all Free Church ministers.

The duchess sided with the Free Church party and was a member of the local congregation at Huntly. When their Communion Season came round, with hundreds coming in from a wide area, she opened the castle park for an open-air service. The result of this was remembered a few years later when the great '59 Revival began to bear fruit in the north-east. It gave Duncan Matheson an idea.

Matheson approached the duchess to ask if a gathering might be held in the park. It would, he believed, benefit many of the new converts who often found themselves isolated in an unsympathetic community. How it would encourage them, he said, if they could meet together. And would not such a large gathering attract the curious and provide another opportunity for outreach? The duchess was hesitant. Some of her friends were unhappy at the idea. It was something new, and no one could be sure in advance what would happen. However, after much prayer and with not a little anxiety she gave her permission.

Thousands flocked to the castle park. The duchess, now thoroughly committed, met all expenses, housed the visiting preachers, and encouraged everyone. She also decided that similar meetings must be held again. Over the next three years as many as 10000 people would attend. Yet despite the great numbers all the rallies were characterised by good order and deep solemnity. The results in changed lives were seen for many years.

Duchess Elizabeth used her wealth in many other ways. She had a particular fondness for children. So at Huntly and in Edinburgh and elsewhere she built schools in memory of her husband.

At the time it had been a difficult decision. She had wanted to live a quiet life but had felt obliged to retain her title and use her position as Duchess of Gordon to do things that a private citizen could not do, and to wield an influence that other people did not possess. For in her particular station there was work to do for the Master and she did it all for him.

Woodrow Wilson
(1856–1924)

2 Corinthians 4:8–9

We are afflicted in every way, but not crushed; perplexed, but not driven to despair; [9]persecuted, but not forsaken; struck down, but not destroyed;

'I feel like going to bed — and staying there.' The President of the United States turned to Dr Grayson, his personal physician. The news was bad. The senate had rejected the treaty for the second time. Woodrow Wilson had worked so hard to establish a just peace in the wake of the First World War. To him the proposed League of Nations offered the best, perhaps the only, hope for the future. He had argued, he had pleaded, he had travelled the country. He had worn himself out. Now, it seemed, his work was in ruins: the senate refused to ratify the treaty.

President Wilson did not go to bed. He asked Dr Grayson to read to him. He asked him to take the Bible and read to him 2 Corinthians 4:8–9. Then he said, 'If I were not a Christian, I think I should go mad. But my faith in God holds me to the belief that he is in some way working out his own plans through human perversities and mistakes.'

From his earliest years Woodrow Wilson had learned to put his trust in God. His father, Joseph Ruggles Wilson, had been a prominent Presbyterian minister, one of the founders — and subsequently Assembly Moderator and Clerk — of the Southern Presbyterian Church. His father, Woodrow's grandfather, had left the family home at Dergalt in County Tyrone to become a newspaper editor in Ohio. The family could trace back their Presbyterian origins to the Reformation. His mother, Janet Woodrow, herself the daughter of a Presbyterian manse, could trace her descent back to a converted priest in Reformation Scotland. Woodrow Wilson was proud of this tradition and knew very well how it influenced his character and personality. Yet his faith, while central to his inheritance, was very much his own.

It was his faith that made him the strictly honourable man he was. Even before he entered politics he showed this quality as President of Princeton University when he resolutely refused to lower standards or change policies to accommodate the rich and powerful. This same sense of honour led him to reject the help of a certain publisher who wanted to support his presidential candidacy. He had a low opinion of him and would not be associated with him — even if it meant losing the nomination. And, of course, there was his crusade for the League of Nations, undertaken against fierce opposition.

It was his faith that made Wilson a reformer. In fact, it was his developing Christian understanding that led him to change his political philosophy. At first he had been unhappy with the idea of government intervention. After all, he was himself an individualist, in politics as in religion. Then his views changed and it was as a Christian that he pushed for social reform. During his 1916 campaign he spoke of his vision of a new society in which the government would protect the weak and root out exploitation.

Wilson lived out his faith at home. For him it was important to set aside time each day to pray and read the Bible. He was always an active churchgoer. At Princeton he served as an elder and at Washington he delighted in being part of the small congregation at Central Presbyterian Church.

It is not surprising then to see Wilson, at a time when everything seemed black, turning to the Bible for the strength he needed. And the help did come. No, there was no fairy-tale happy ending — the United States did not join the League, and Wilson's own health did not recover from the stress and strain — but there was a peace.

John Stevenson
(1655–1728)

2 Corinthians 5:20

So we are ambassadors for Christ, God making his appeal through us. We beseech you on behalf of Christ, be reconciled to God.

Curiosity, we say, killed the cat. It nearly did as much for John Stevenson. Certainly it was curiosity that drew this farmer's son to the hall of Killochan Castle. He came to hear an outlawed preacher, Thomas Kennedy, and he came specifically because Kennedy was an outlawed preacher. Young John Stevenson wanted to know what was so different about this man and his message. So he walked the short distance along the Girvan valley from his father's farm at Camregan to the castle. And he heard Kennedy.

What he heard upset him. It was the first time he had felt the power of God's Word in his heart and he found it an upsetting experience. Now he knew he had a soul to be saved. So he began to look for answers to the questions that were troubling him. And the answer came twice!

The first time was in the churchyard at Kirkmichael where another of these outlawed preachers spoke on 2 Corinthians 5:20. Shortly afterwards Stevenson heard the same text again at another conventicle, held outside the town of Maybole at Craigdow Hill where the preacher was John Welsh (grandson of Welsh of Ayr). This time the message really did strike home and Stevenson said, 'With all my heart and soul I did cordially and cheerfully make the offer welcome.' From that day, 12 August 1678, John Stevenson was a different person.

Years later he wrote it all down in a little book that is still in print today. The title reflects Stevenson's style as a writer, and his concern as an author, for his book is called *A Rare Soul-Strengthening and Comforting Cordial for Old and Young Christians*. It is known more simply as *A Comforting Cordial*.

In a sense the book is an adventure story. For Stevenson took his stand alongside those preachers who had first made him think seriously about the Gospel. He joined the Covenanters and, utterly convinced of the rightness of the cause, he marched with the men of Carrick to join the others who had gathered outside Hamilton. There, at Bothwell Brig, the Covenanter forces were scattered. The battle quickly became a rout. Stevenson's companion was killed. For the next nine years Stevenson was a fugitive.

These were dangerous days. Frequent searches were made for Stevenson. The authorities were anxious to catch someone who had been in arms, and money could be earned by those willing to betray outlaw Covenanters. Stevenson remarked grimly that 'there were many informers in the country.'

Several times he was almost caught. Once he himself opened the door of the farmhouse, and found three dragoons on the doorstep. He kept calm and they rode off after taking some food. Afterwards they realised their mistake and came back, but John Stevenson was long gone. They were going to seize his father for sheltering a fugitive — a very serious offence — but the old man told them that he would report to their officer that they had let their man escape. So they released him.

On a later occasion he just escaped by hiding in the garden. This nearly proved fatal, for some of the soldiers wanted to try the blackberries in the garden, the very place where Stevenson was concealed. The father managed to persuade them that the berries were full of worms and settled them in at the table for a meal while John slipped away to the hills.

It was a sore struggle to survive. One winter he lived in a haystack. Many a night he bedded down in the local graveyard. And all the time his family were subject to harassment. His wife was arrested but she refused to say anything and she was later released by a party of friends who got her out at night.

Yet the book is more concerned with Stevenson's inner struggles. It is therefore of even more interest, for it not only tells us what happened to the ordinary Convenanters during those years, but also it shows us what they thought and felt.

To a modern reader Stevenson may appear to be too inward looking, too concerned with his doubts and fears. Yet there is no doubting the reality of the struggle nor the strength of the faith which eventually carried him through. In his later years he would often walk over to Kirkoswald and spend the day in the church in prayer and meditation. His advice to his children was 'Set apart some time every day for reading God's Word; read it with

observation, depending on God to make it useful to your souls.'
Here then is the secret of Stevenson's victory. Through many real
dangers and through many sore doubts he battled on because he
knew where to turn for help.

God had spoken to him at Craigdow Hill. There and then he
had found reconciliation and peace. Over the next ten and more
years his faith was to be tried and tested, but Stevenson was kept
safe, and he found his strength in the study of God's word.

A D Grant
(1853–1914)

Galatians 6:2

Bear one another's burdens, and so fulfil the law of Christ.

'Came to Greenock for good this evening by 6.5 train from St Enoch's.' Alexander Duncan Grant wrote that in his diary on 12 September 1883. He had arrived in town as minister of the small Free Church congregation of Mount Park. And there he did stay — for good.

He was in many ways a remarkable man, this A D Grant. True, he never became famous, not even in the way some ministers become famous. Yet Professor Mackintosh once said that if all the different Churches in Scotland were to be judged by one representative — one man or woman to show them at their best — then for his Church he would choose A D Grant of Greenock and 'have no fear of the result'.

Grant actually came from Cullen and he first went to work as an office boy in Dundee. Then, to study for the ministry, he came to Glasgow. From there, as we've seen, he took the train to his first and only charge at Mount Park.

What made him so special? A mixture of things, I suppose. For one thing, he was a sound scholar and a hard worker who turned out the kind of sermons that made you think. Whether you wanted to or not. He was a serious man, old-fashioned in his views even then. But — like his great friend J P Struthers — he had a mischievous sense of humour. Like the time when he introduced himself to a rather clever young minister newly arrived in town. 'I'm Grant,' he said, 'No doubt you're familiar with my books.' He hadn't written any!

He was also a very kind man, recklessly generous. It was not at all uncommon for him to give away his coat. Literally off his back. But he gave more than that: he gave himself. To the poor of the town, to the destitute; he liked to help those who couldn't do much to help themselves. And, best of all, he did it quietly and cheerfully. Just like his Master.

Grant enjoyed his sport. When he had the time, which wasn't often, he and Struthers liked to watch cricket and they played their own version of golf. Grant, a left-hander, was expert at putting. A few choice friends who were on the same wavelength would usually join in. You see, there was nothing unhealthy or unnatural about Grant's religion, strict though it was. He wasn't the least bit sour. And he was very approachable. Anyone could talk to him, tramps and children, professors and industrialists. He treated them all with the same kindness, though he was not to be taken in by specious rogues.

When he was a student, preaching his trial sermon before Professor Candlish, he didn't do so very well. Professor Candlish didn't let that sort of thing go. He told young Grant what he thought and then — for he was a kind man — he added 'but I'm sure you will write a better sermon on that text'. Now the text in question was Galatians 6:2, and Grant did most certainly write a better sermon on that text. He wrote it with his life. His whole ministry was a living out of those words.

A few days before he died, he saw a message boy struggling with a heavy basket. Perhaps it was because he always remembered his own days as an office boy running errands, perhaps it was just his natural kindness, but Grant was ever quick to help young folk. So he stepped forward and taking the lad's basket carried it for him. He carried it all the way, even although for him it was the wrong way.

When two of his friends were talking about this little incident and saying how like Grant it was, one of them said, 'Yes, and he carried a lot of our burdens too.' He was the one they went to, for advice, for guidance, for comfort. His great friend Struthers wrote a wonderful children's magazine called *The Morning Watch*. He wrote it himself while his wife drew the pictures. But while he was happy to turn to all his friends for ideas and suggestions it was to Grant that he turned the most. And never in vain. In this, as in everything, he wanted neither recognition nor applause. It was enough that he could be of help.

A D Grant, the quiet scholar, the thoughtful preacher, the cheery companion, the old-fashioned great heart who went round doing good — a favourite little thing was to clear orange peel from the pavement wherever he walked — right to the end he was the burden bearer. It's a good way for anyone to be remembered.

J C Ryle
(1816–1900)

Ephesians 2:8
> For by grace you have been saved through faith; and this is not your
> own doing, it is the gift of God —

He might have been Mayor of Macclesfield. He was Bishop of
Liverpool. He might have been a business man and a banker. He
was a clergyman and a writer. He might have been a famous
Member of Parliament. He was a noted controversialist. He was
John Charles Ryle.

His father, another John, was mayor. He was a prominent
figure in and around Macclesfield, living in a large house on Park
Green, owning mills and farms and latterly running a bank.
When a son was born in 1816 it seemed that here was the heir to
the family business empire.

Certainly John Charles Ryle was given an education fitting his
station. After time at a private school he went on to Eton and,
from there, to Oxford. At school he became cricket captain and
learned to row. He didn't like every aspect of school life but
concluded that it taught him that he wouldn't always get things
his own way. That was to prove a valuable lesson.

At Oxford, Ryle at first paid more attention to sports and to
dancing than he did to his studies, but he then settled down to
hard work and took a double first. During these years, both at
home and at school and university, he attended church. He had
been well grounded in the essentials of the faith but, as yet, had
no personal knowledge of Jesus as Saviour and Lord.

Then one Sunday he was, as usual, in church. It was not a
particularly memorable service. In fact, Ryle remembered almost
nothing about it, not even the sermon. One thing, however, did
stay with him. The second lesson came from Ephesians 2. The
reader — Ryle didn't know who he was — read the passage slowly
and gave special emphasis to verse 8, pausing between each clause.

That did it. What no sermon had said, what no liturgy had

conveyed, came to him in the simple reading of the Word. Through that verse read in church John Charles Ryle was brought into saving relationship with Jesus.

He had no one to turn to for advice. But he did have books to help him. He also had his early grounding in the 39 Articles of his Church. Here he found the help he needed. He repaid that debt. For he himself became a prolific writer, his books and tracts helping others, and he became a doughty champion of the Evangelical tradition of the English Church. But not yet. No, his new-found faith had not suggested a change of plan. Rather he seemed all set to join the family business.

After some experience at Lincoln's Inn, Ryle went to work in his father's bank. He also became a magistrate and a captain in the Cheshire Yeomanry. His father had entered parliament and, from his showing at a local political meeting, it seemed that here too young John was preparing to follow in his father's footsteps.

Then the bank collapsed. With it went the family fortune, the house, the servants, almost everything. They felt it keenly, this sudden devastating change in their fortunes. Ryle once said that only his faith kept him from suicide. But they could not sit around feeling sorry for themselves. John had to find something to do. At first he thought of becoming a private secretary to a politician and he nearly attached himself to Gladstone, then a man very obviously on the way up. But Ryle felt no confidence in him. That door closed. The one that opened was in the Church. On 12 December 1841 Ryle was ordained at Farnham Castle as a clergyman of the English Church. It should not be thought that he had taken on this work as a last resort. Rather, he came to see that God, having ended the career that he had always thought inevitable, was calling him to full-time service.

His first post was at Exbury in the New Forest. 'Dreary, desolate and solitary', he called it. Unhealthy too. But Ryle was undaunted. To his labours in the pulpit he added much-needed practical help in the parish and acted, unofficially but effectively, as a doctor! His days in Exbury took their toll, however. His own health suffered, and so he felt he had to move on.

Ryle went to Helmingham in Suffolk and, after 17 years there, moved to another rural charge, Stradbroke, in 1861. During these years in the country he showed himself to be an energetic pastor and a gifted preacher. He also began to write, his writing characterised by simple language and a direct style. An Ipswich printer agreed to join in a publishing enterprise and for some 50 years Ryle turned out a flood of tracts and over 30 books. These included his *Expository Thoughts on the Gospels*, so prized by Spurgeon, and still so popular today.

In 1880 Ryle received a telegram summoning him to London to meet the Prime Minister. To his surprise he was asked to go to Liverpool as the first bishop of the city. By then he was 64, well-known and deeply respected as one of the leading men in his Church, the champion of the Evangelical party. For the next 20 years Ryle worked in the city and diocese with all his old vigour, taking the opportunity whenever possible to speak and act on behalf of many societies and organisations. At the same time his publications continued to appear: it was reckoned that more than 12 million copies of his tracts were sold with another million or so being translated into some 12 languages.

As one writer remarked, 'Few Christians have lived a more influential life and few have left writings of such enduring value.'

Augustus Toplady
(1740–1778)

Ephesians 2:13

But now in Christ Jesus you who once were far off have been brought near in the blood of Christ.

'I shall remember that day to all eternity.' That day in the barn. A rather ordinary barn, too, in a remote corner of County Wexford. That was where Augustus Toplady met and heard James Morris.

Toplady was 16 at the time, and he was on holiday. He heard that a service was to be held in a barn not far from where he was staying. The preacher, it was said, was one of these Methodist folk, an uneducated man who yet had a way of getting through to his hearers. Augustus felt that this would be worth hearing. Not everyone agreed with him and there were only a few in the barn that night.

The preacher, James Morris, spoke to the text Ephesians 2:13. And the words seized hold of Toplady. The simple Gospel sermon of the preacher brought home to him, as no other sermon had ever done, the love of Jesus. That night Toplady gave his life to the Saviour.

He afterwards said that he thought it strange that this same message had never come to him at a church service. He therefore determined that the Gospel would be heard whenever he took a service. For he knew now what his life's work had to be. After graduating from Trinity College in Dublin, he entered the ministry of the Church of England in 1762. Some time later he was appointed vicar of Broadhembury in Devon.

From the first he drew the crowds with the passion and power of his preaching. And soon there was another poet in print.

In 1776, the year after he moved to London as the minister of a French Calvinist congregation, he published what was to become his most celebrated poem. At this time he was acting as editor of *The Gospel Magazine*, and in the March edition he wrote an article on the national debt, drawing what he called 'spiritual improvement' from the situation. At the end of the piece he included a four-verse poem: 'Rock of Ages'.

This poem has caused considerable argument. While some say that Toplady wrote these lines when caught in a storm and forced to shelter in a cave, and identify the very spot in a limestone gorge at Burrington Combe in Somerset, and tell of a playing card that Toplady found there and on which he first wrote these words — a card which is now housed in a museum in America — others say it never happened. No, they argue, Toplady was always fascinated by the idea of Jesus as the Rock of Ages, and the poem was simply the best expression he gave to this idea and was not inspired by any one incident.

Of course, in a sense, it doesn't really matter. What matters is that Augustus Toplady wrote these lines and these lines have been sung ever since. A C Benson once wrote, 'To have written words which should come home to people in moments of high, deep, and passionate emotion, consecrating, consoling, uplifting ... there can hardly be anything better worth doing than that.' He was writing about Toplady and this hymn.

Not that this was the only thing he ever wrote. Other hymns that still survive include 'A debtor to mercy alone' and 'A Sovereign Protector I have'. Most of his many pamphlets — though a few are still in print — have not survived. He and John Wesley exchanged some hard knocks in a dispute which shows neither man at his best.

A man who believes as intensely as Toplady — or as Wesley — will often be impatient of disagreement. And Toplady had not much time. He wore himself out with his work, making no attempt to conserve his strength, and died at 38.

Yet the image of fierce controversialist and fervent preacher can be rather misleading, for there was a gentle side to Toplady, seen in his hymns. For example, the hymn 'Your harps, ye trembling saints' was written specifically for 'weak believers' to encourage them. Toplady understood their fears. In the original version of 'A Sovereign Protector I have', written in 1767, he contrasts our weakness with our Protector's unfailing care. He knew how far short we all fall.

Augustus Toplady first met his Friend and Protector in a barn in Ireland. That Friend stayed with him and Toplady was happy to expend himself in telling others about the One who is the Rock of Ages.

Emily Prankard
(*c*1822–1885)

Philippians 1:21
For to me to live is Christ, and to die is gain.

'She is a jolly kind of body,' he wrote, 'and does not take offence.'
In fact, he told his friend, 'She is a good lassie ... and just as
handy as a Scotch lass would have been.' Thus James Gilmour
described his new wife.

Emily Prankard was undoubtedly an unusual lady. She had
sailed to China to marry a man she had never seen. His first letter
to her had contained his proposal. True, she had heard something
about him because James Gilmour, Gilmour of Mongolia, was
already known in Church circles for his missionary exploits. And,
anyway, was he not the trusted colleague and dear friend of her
own sister's husband, S E Meech? That was how he had first
found out about her, when he had seen her photograph on top of
Mrs Meech's harmonium.

So here she was, leaving her home, her mother and her work at
Bexley Heath to sail round the world to meet and marry a man she
had never met. She must have been a jolly body. Her first glimpse
of her husband-to-be cannot have been too reassuring. He and
Meech had come to meet her off the boat at Tientsin. He was
wearing an old and rather grubby overcoat and was muffled
against the morning cold in an ancient woollen scarf. Everyone on
board thought he was an engineer.

The following spring Emily set out with her husband for
Mongolia. They travelled by ox-cart and they slept in a cloth tent.
It was not a smooth journey. She found the food — a diet of millet
and mutton — difficult to eat. She found the lack of privacy
irksome, for the Mongols were fascinated and would allow them
no privacy, not even to wash. A month on the road and they were
caught in a terrible storm. The cart was overturned, the tents
were ripped, their bedding soaked. Yet Emily stayed jolly. She
was a delicate and refined lady but she bore all the hardship and

privation cheerfully. 'She is a better missionary than I,' confessed her husband.

Emily went on two more expeditions, surviving another near disaster in which they were almost swept away in a flood. Then, with the arrival of the children, she settled for life inside the Peking mission. Not that this was uneventful. Lack of accommodation led her quick-tempered husband into a row with another missionary, Dr John Dudgeon. Gilmour had commandeered as a study a room previously used by Dudgeon as a medical store and book depot. The row turned into a protracted feud that dragged on for years. It was as well that Emily did not take offence easily.

She herself had plenty to do, apart from looking after Gilmour and the children. She worked with the Chinese women and girls. She had been a teacher at home and now she used her skills and experience to help the educational side of the mission. She also took her turn at the harmonium on Sundays.

Emily had impressed the Mongols during those earlier tours. She had learned their language and that had pleased them. She had also shown a fondness for animals and was obviously a caring person. They liked her. So too did the Chinese in Peking. Unquestionably she played an important part in helping the work advance. How sad it then was that she was unable to do much when the work suddenly began to expand.

The truth was her health had been failing for some years. There were prolonged bouts of pain and recovery was slow. Emily faced the facts bravely. She wrote to her sister, 'I can't get stronger. So I must be content to be tired.'

She carried on doing whatever she could but by August it was clear that she was seriously ill. James Gilmour was desolate. Theirs had been the happiest of marriages. He could hardly bear to think of life without Emily. One Sunday evening they sat together. 'Well, Jamie,' she said, 'I'm going, I suppose. I'll see you soon there. It won't be long.' He said she wouldn't miss him much, not there. She smiled. 'I think I'll sit at the gate and look for you coming.' Within the week, he wrote to friends, 'she had crossed the river'.

Through these years in China Emily had kept a text from Philippians 1 on her wall. James Gilmour once asked her if she really believed in its words. Yes, she said, she did. During that last illness she was eager to get better but only for his sake and for the children. For herself she was happy to know that there was a Friend waiting and, for her, the river held no fears.

Henry Sidgwick
(1838–1900)

Philippians 3:12–14

Not that I have already obtained this or am already perfect; but I press on to make it my own, because Christ Jesus has made me his own. [13]Brethren, I do not consider that I have made it my own; but one thing I do, forgetting what lies behind and straining forward to what lies ahead, [14]I press on toward the goal for the prize of the upward call of God in Christ Jesus.

Henry Sidgwick. No, I don't suppose the name rings any bells. At one time he was well-enough known. At least in some circles. But by now he's very much forgotten. Even in Cambridge.

It was there he made his reputation. It was back in May 1838 that Henry Sidgwick was born in the Yorkshire town of Skipton where his father was schoolmaster. A bright lad was Henry. He went to school at Rugby and from there he passed to Cambridge. Here, at Trinity College, he discovered the great passion of his life: moral philosophy.

In 1874 at the age of 36 he wrote his book. Not his first book, you understand, but the one that made him famous. It was called *Methods of Ethics*. His old university made him a lecturer on the strength of it, and in 1883 he was appointed Professor of Moral Philosophy.

These were busy years for Professor Sidgwick. He lectured and he wrote. He had a lot to say about economics and politics too. His reputation grew. He became interested in the higher education of women and was one of the first to champion the right of women to a place in the universities.

Yes, a busy man, a public-spirited man. Good at what he did and happy doing it.

His wife tells us why. An interesting girl herself, the sister of a Prime Minister (A J Balfour), she tells us about her Henry and his Bible.

Professor Sidgwick was a Christian, a convinced Christian, who took his Bible seriously. And this is what he did. . . .

At different times in his life, at various points in his career, he turned to the Bible and searched for a text that might serve as a motto — a word that would help him from day to day. He did this for himself, looking for and finding the right word, the word he needed, for this time, for these days.

During the height of his career, when he was so very busy, he kept this word before him: Philippians 3:12–14 and in particular verse 13.

It's a very interesting choice. Clearly, for Henry Sidgwick, it worked. He could so easily have looked behind: at his work, his success, his wealth, his position. He could have rested on his laurels. But he didn't. He had more to give and, as a Christian, he knew he had to go on giving. So he pressed on, ever on.

It is easy to look back. Too easy. To sit down and count up all we've done — or think we've done — for the Church, for God. Easy, too, is looking around, watching the others. Not too impressive, are they? We've done so much more, or suffered so much more, or done it so much better. It's easy, too easy, to tell ourselves to sit back and let the others do a bit for a change. It's easy to look back and grow complacent. Or bitter. That happens. We can look back and feel that no one has ever understood what we've done. We've never got the credit we deserve.

Henry Sidgwick didn't look back. He listened to Paul. 'I'm not perfect,' said Paul. No false modesty here. Not with this man. 'I've still a long way to go. So — for the Master's sake — I'll press on.' The picture here is of the athlete pounding round the track. The tape is still out in front. The race isn't over yet. It has still to be won. Or lost. So he doesn't look back. He doesn't look to the side. He looks ahead. And keeps on going.

That's what Paul did. 'Here's something else to do', he'd say, 'more folk to see, more letters to write. Let's keep going.'

Henry Sidgwick kept going, giving his best all the way.

Isn't that what Jesus says to us? 'Never mind the others. And never mind what you've done. Don't look back. Don't look to the side. Look ahead. There's still more to do. So — press on — and win the prize.'

Sir Wilfred Grenfell
(1865–1940)

2 Timothy 1:12

And therefore I suffer as I do. But I am not ashamed, for I know whom I have believed, and I am sure that he is able to guard until that Day what has been entrusted to me.

It might never have happened if it hadn't been for the young lad off the training ship. If he hadn't stood up when he did. . . .

They knighted Wilfred Grenfell in 1927. By then his was a household name: Grenfell of Labrador. That's what they called him, and with good reason too. The story was well known, that of a young doctor sailing off in a small ketch to Newfoundland, a ketch he had had fitted out as a hospital ship. It was a bold venture and it had brought, in time, great results. Eventually there were six hospitals and four hospital ships. And the schools, the orphanages, the stores, and the missions, all part of the work he started. Grenfell — a tireless missionary, a devoted doctor and an able propagandist — won the respect and affection of the tough fisherman who worked the banks. He also won a special place among the Eskimos. Back home in England he was a hero.

Yet that night he had been afraid. He had wanted to stand up. All those who had decided to follow Christ Jesus were asked to stand. No one moved. It was a very mixed audience there in east London. The speaker was a great cricketing hero, one of a number of Christian sportsmen who had come to the East End to preach the Gospel. Their fame drew the crowds, among them Wilfred Grenfell and some of his friends.

As he listened, Grenfell knew that the time had come for him to decide. He had never before heard the challenge of the Gospel. Not like this. Now he realised that the only truly satisfying life, the only life worth living, was the life of Christian service. He wanted to stand up. But he couldn't. He was a medical student with his reputation to consider. And his friends were there.

Then the boy from the training ship stood up. There were

about 100 of these boys, sitting at the front in their sailor shirts, a tough bunch who were only there because they had been told to go. One of them stood up. In front of his mates. He was only a small lad, too, but he stood up. Grenfell could guess what that would cost the boy when he got back on board. Yet he stood up.

Courage was always a quality Grenfell admired. As a boy he saw it in his sporting heroes and he was to remain a firm believer in the value of games. He once ran a boxing class for his Sunday School. It was a quality he saw in the fishermen. He sometimes said that he was himself of seafaring stock and took pride in being a descendant of the Elizabethan sea-dogs. Courage was very important to Grenfell.

At one time it had almost turned him against Christianity. There were those who made Christianity seem something soft and useless, all right for the chapel and the sick room, all right for girls and vicars. This, he felt, could not be right. He himself came to see Jesus as the bravest as well as the kindest, and his way as the hardest as well as the best. And that realisation brought another problem. What if he, Wilfred Grenfell, was after all not brave enough? He knew there would be many difficulties and dangers and, while he welcomed them in prospect and said the adventure of going to Labrador to pioneer work was 'almost too good to be true', yet what if it all got too much for him, what then?

Wilfred Grenfell found his answer in the Bible, in a verse from 2 Timothy. That verse told him that it wasn't up to Wilfred Grenfell; there was a strength that was greater than his own. As an old man he said that he could still quote this verse without hesitation, for it had often helped him and was still a source of strength.

David Dickson
(*c* 1583–1662)

2 Peter 3:15–16

And count the forbearance of our Lord as salvation. So also our beloved brother Paul wrote to you according to the wisdom given him, [16]speaking of this as he does in all his letters. There are some things in them hard to understand, which the ignorant and unstable twist to their own destruction, as they do the other scriptures.

Shakespeare's Mark Anthony would have it that 'The evil that men do lives after them.' Sometimes it is worse. Sometimes men are remembered for the evil they did not do. Such was David Dickson. He is often mentioned in histories of the Covenanting period for something that he really never said. When, it is alleged, the Irish prisoners were slaughtered after the Battle of Philiphaugh in 1645, a Covenanter preacher is supposed to have remarked with glee, 'The work goes bonnily on.' Dickson is usually said to be that preacher.

In fact the evidence is highly suspect. The source of the story is Henry Guthry. And Guthry is something less than totally reliable when it comes to telling the truth about his former colleagues.

But Dickson was a good target. He was at that time one of the most prominent and most respected of the Covenanter ministers, the ideal person to accuse. A merchant's son, brought up in Glasgow, he had gone to his native university and from there he had moved to Irvine as minister in 1618.

From the first he was involved in controversy. Refusing to accept the Five Articles of Perth which, he felt, had been imposed on the Church by the king and passed by a hand-picked assembly, he was deprived of his charge and banished to Turriff. Thanks to the intervention of the sympathetic Earl of Eglinton, he was able to return after only one year in 'exile', and came home in time to take a leading part in the revival that had broken out in the neighbouring village of Stewarton. 'The Stewarton Sickness' some had called it, but it proved to be a genuine movement and many lives were changed throughout the district and beyond. Market days in Irvine gave Dickson a great opportunity to reach the crowds, their numbers now swollen with the curious and the sceptical. He took that opportunity. Years later an English merchant, recalling his preaching, said, 'He showed me all my heart'.

Dickson showed he had a unique talent for this work. On Sunday evenings his manse was opened to troubled souls seeking help. As many as 20 would come of an evening and he had time for them all. Out of these experiences came a book, Dickson's manual for counsellors, his *Therapeutica Sacra*.

It was at this time that the National Covenant was drawn up and copies sent round the country for signing. Dickson was one of those chosen to accompany the Covenant to Aberdeen in an effort to 'sell' it in that Episcopal stronghold. The mission did not succeed, but Dickson's part was noted.

The next year — 1639 — saw him chosen as Moderator of the General Assembly. There he spoke to the members, urging them, 'Love one another; strive not, neither insult over those that be of a discrepant judgment from us.' Which doesn't sound like Guthry's blood-thirsty fanatic.

After a brief spell as an army chaplain, Dickson was then called back to his old university to act as Professor of Divinity. Joined the next year by another Ayrshire minister, the immortal diarist Robert Baillie, the Glasgow school 'entered one of its great periods'. During his time there he made friends with James Durham, a friendship which would prove very important.

One of the most important things Dickson did in these years at Glasgow, and during his subsequent stay at Edinburgh, was to begin writing his Bible commentaries. As he explained it himself, there was a crying need for 'short and plain' books to help promote intelligent Bible reading among ordinary folk. Such books would also silence the 'witty sluggard' who claimed to be too busy. The idea was fine and everyone said so. But no one did any writing. So, to get things started, to show what might be done, Dickson took up his own pen.

He chose the Epistle to the Hebrews. He chose it because he thought it a 'hard piece of meat'. Some modern scholars might not share Dickson's conviction that Paul wrote Hebrews and some may wish to question the authorship of 2 Peter. No matter. Dickson's point is quite clear: some books of the Bible are harder to understand than others; the Bible itself says so. Very well, he will start with a book that is known to be difficult. Then others, thus encouraged, would carry on 'with more hope of success'.

Dickson's plan worked. Not only did he produce a book of solid worth, not only did he himself go on to write other commentaries — notably on Matthew and the Psalms — he also inspired others to try their hand. Men such as George Hutcheson, Alexander Nisbet, James Fergusson, and his old friend James Durham all contributed to what became a distinct school of commentating. Their books, it is interesting to see, won the warm approval of Spurgeon and remain in print today.

So does *The Sum of Saving Knowledge* which Dickson wrote up from a series of sermons he once preached at Inveraray. Durham helped him put it together. This, too, has had a lasting effect on Scottish Church life. For example, in 1834 a study of its pages proved to be an all-important event for a young man called Robert Murray McCheyne in his search for assurance.

So Dickson was right. By tackling a difficult task himself he did encourage others. The same could also be said of his life: by facing up to the challenge of the day, by braving persecution, by staying true when others did not, he helped the people of his time by his example. And in this way he can help people still.

Frances Ridley Havergal
(1836–1879)

1 John 1:7

But if we walk in the light, as he is in the light, we have fellowship
with one another, and the blood of Jesus his Son cleanses us from all
sin.

Frances was the baby of the family. When she was born in
December 1836 there were already three girls and two boys in the
rector's home. They were a happy and loving family and the little
girl was a favourite with them all. They were a clever family, too,
with the father, William Henry Havergal, becoming famous for
his work with Church music.

Young Frances inherited her share of this talent. She could
read at four, wrote poetry at seven, went on to master five languages, and excelled at the piano. Yet over this happy home and
gifted family there hung a cloud. When Frances was only 11 her
mother died. The father was injured in a road accident and for a
time there were fears he might never work again. Frances herself
was a delicate child and doctors advised against further study. To
add to this there was her fear of God. As a child of six she had
been frightened by a sermon (not one of her father's) on hell and
judgment. She talked to no one about her fears and for years that
sermon haunted her. Ill health and family sorrows added to her
troubles and she became morbidly fascinated with death.

Then, at the age of 13, she went to school at Belmont. Under
the influence of the teacher and the school chaplain, a number of
girls were led to a personal faith. Seeing their happiness Frances
longed to share their faith and know their peace of mind. But
somehow she felt that she wouldn't ever enjoy the assurance they
had.

She confided in a friend and the two of them talked together.
Sitting one night on the drawing room sofa, deep in talk, Frances
found the light breaking. She went to her room and there, on her
knees, she gave her life to Jesus. From that night on her life was

filled with joy, the joy of serving Jesus. Her favourite way of talking about Jesus was to call him Master. Having found his love she now wanted to show her love for him by serving him as Master.

In July 1854 she was confirmed as a member of the English Church in Worcester Cathedral. That night she wrote a short poem which she entitled 'Thine For Ever'. And that was to be her work. She did do other things — she was much involved in Sunday School teaching and in various charities — but when ill health forced her to rest she kept on writing.

A number of well-loved hymns were written by Frances. Perhaps the best-known and certainly the most characteristic, was the one she wrote in 1874. The words came to her as she lay in bed unable to sleep. The next day she wrote them down and they were published four years later, ever since when we have been singing 'Take my life and let it be Consecrated, Lord, to Thee'. More than any other of her hymns it expresses Frances' happy faith and loving service.

Together with the religious verse that she wrote there also appeared an immensely popular series of little books. Under titles such as *The Four Happy Days, Morning Stars, The Royal Invitation* and *Loyal Responses*, she brought comfort and inspiration to many people. It wasn't just what she wrote, it was the winsome cheerfulness with which she expressed herself that made her books so popular. They revealed a sympathetic heart too. And this fact led on to another activity that was to mean much for Frances.

People started to write to her. They wrote because they had read one of her books and felt that here was someone who would understand their problems, who would be able to help. So began her work as a counsellor. Of course, there was never anything official about this work, nothing organised. It was simply that people kept on writing and Frances always made the time to write back. It was all part of the service which she wanted to give.

Until her last illness, which came in 1879, Frances continued to write with all her old sweetness. Nothing, it seemed, could sour her nature nor shake her faith. She delighted in her Bible: 'If only one searches,' she once said, 'there are such extraordinary things in the Bible.' She found many of them. But there was one verse which she called 'my own text'.

1 John 1:7 was very precious to her. As she explained it, she

came to see one Sunday afternoon that if we will but give ourselves completely to Jesus he will keep us clean from sin. It is sin, she said, that causes our doubts and threatens our relationship with Jesus. So to escape from that anxiety we have only to put ourselves wholly into his hands, and he will keep us. Full surrender will lead to full blessedness.

As the end drew near Frances was peaceful. When told that there was no hope of recovery she said, 'Then it's home the faster.' And to the watching family she confided, 'So beautiful to go.' She asked that one text be put on her stone. Yes, it was her text, the one that had led her to a deeper commitment and a stronger faith, the one that had brought her such peace.

Sarah Burgess
(*c*1785–1856)

1 John 1:9
> If we confess our sins, he is faithful and just, and will forgive our sins and cleanse us from all unrighteousness.

Sitting there in the third-class smoking compartment of the Norwich to Liverpool train, the men fell easily into conversation. The two soldiers told their companion about a trip they had made some years ago. They had gone down to London to see the sights. They had been anxious to make the most of their day and so they were rather late by the time they reached Westminster Abbey. The doors were just being closed. They were turning away in disappointment when a stranger spoke to them.

Could they possibly come back the next day, he asked. That, they replied, was impossible. The stranger then turned to the beadle and, after a few words, took his keys, unlocked the door, and invited the two friends in. The stranger, it turned out, was Arthur Stanley, Dean of Westminster.

The dean, who loved the abbey, took great delight in showing the soldiers round. As they came back to the door he remarked that it was a great thing to be commemorated in the abbey among so many famous and noble names. Then he said something strange. 'Yet', he said, 'you may both have an even better monument than this.' They looked at the dean in astonishment. 'These, even these,' he said, 'will one day moulder into dust. But you can live for ever. If,' he added, 'your names are written in the Lamb's Book of Life.'

Not surprisingly, these words stayed with the two soldiers. That chance encounter proved to be a turning point in their lives. But then Dean Stanley influenced many people. In many ways. He was a controversial figure in his time as dean. Among the best-known preachers in the country, he was also a prolific writer. His opinions were eagerly sought and fiercely debated. Yes, most certainly, he did influence many people.

There had been many influences on his life. There were his parents, his father being a well-known Bishop of Norwich. There was Dr Arnold at Rugby. Arthur Stanley was said to have been his favourite pupil and Arnold's influence comes across in the biography of his old teacher that Stanley wrote. Then there was Tait at Oxford. And, of course, there was his wife, the remarkable Lady Augusta Bruce, daughter of the Earl of Elgin and close friend of the Queen.

Yet there was one other influence, one other person who profoundly affected Arthur Stanley and helped — perhaps even more than these others — to make him the man he was. This was Sarah Burgess, his old nurse. She had stayed on with the family for 38 years and, to the last, it was to her that he turned for help and encouragement. 'It was,' he wrote, 'always instructive to hear her talk.' He knew many wise men and some good ones, but Sarah held a special place; she was 'a constant refreshment and support.'

There were a few storms in Stanley's career, even before he became dean. After his appointment, his liberal broad churchmanship led him into conflict with both wings of the Church. He stood his ground with great spirit. Sometimes, it must be admitted, he seemed to take up unpopular causes simply because their unpopularity appealed to his sense of chivalry. He was always an enthusiastic friend of underdogs. His position at Westminster gave him an unusual degree of freedom to go his own way. So he did.

There were times when the strain of battle was excessive, times when 'The heavens seemed black around us.' In such times he would turn to old Sarah or, in later years, to her memory. She never failed to lift his spirits.

Sarah's own serenity came from her faith. Her favourite text was 1 John 1:9. On what turned out to be his last visit, Stanley and she talked about that text. 'God is faithful and just,' that was the ground of her hope, the source of her peace. She needed no more than that. This faith in a faithful and just God made her 'one of the best persons I have ever known'. And through her influence he in turn was able to influence others; her strength and wisdom helped him, so that he in turn was able to help others.

James Chalmers
(1841–1901)

Revelation 22:17

The Spirit and the Bride say, 'Come.' And let him who hears say, 'Come.' And let him who is thirsty come, let him who desires take the water of life without price.

'Your photograph is on my chimney shelf as large as life.' And that was large enough. 'Big, stout, wildish-looking,' was how his friend described him. This friend had an eye for appearance and a neat way of conveying his impression. Robert Louis Stevenson could make a character come alive in the fewest and simplest words. Not that the man in the photograph was lacking in vitality. James Chalmers was a giant of a man, with a great mop of unruly hair, a bushy beard, and 'bold black eyes'. He did not look the least bit like a missionary.

Yet James Chalmers was a missionary, one of the most famous and one of the most loved of all Scottish missionaries. Stevenson had a high regard for Chalmers and he helps us understand the man's appeal. His comments are all the more striking because, as he admitted, he had himself gone to the South Seas with 'a great prejudice against missions'. Chalmers, he said, had 'no humbug, plenty courage, and the love of adventure'; 'A man nobody can see and not love.'

Chalmers spent ten years on Rarotonga. He had adventures enough to fill a book just getting there. And his time on the island was sufficiently difficult as Chalmers led the fight against drunkenness and violence. Yet all the time there he was fretting to go further, to reach those who had never yet heard the Gospel. In 1878 he got his wish and sailed for New Guinea to begin work among the cannibals.

At one time Chalmers' work in New Guinea was as well known as that of Livingstone in Africa. He wrote two books describing his adventures, and when on leave at home he was a thrilling platform speaker, drawing huge crowds. Alexander Gammie, who was something of an expert sermon-taster, once wrote that he had never heard anything so overwhelming as Chalmers' peroration.

And the work, the hard, brave work, was crowned with a martyr's death. Chalmers went ashore on Goaribari Island with a young colleague called Tomkins. They were invited for a meal and while offguard were clubbed and stabbed. They were then beheaded and their bodies eaten the same day. They died on Easter Monday 1901.

The story had begun in August 1841 at Ardrishaig on Loch Fyne. After school the young James Chalmers went to work in a lawyers' office in Inveraray. He was a bit of a handful in those days, full of energy and mischief. However, he still attended Sunday School and it was there, sitting in the vestry in the United Presbyterian Church, that his heart was touched and his imagination fired as the minister read a letter from a missionary in Fiji. On his way home, at the back of a wall beside the bridge over the Aray Water, he knelt down and prayed that one day God would make him a missionary to the cannibals.

It was a prayer that did not seem likely to be answered in the way Chalmers had asked. For he himself took a 'scunner' at religion and began to run around with a rough crowd. When they heard that two evangelists from Ireland had been invited to conduct services in Inveraray, they decided that this was not for them, unless they could find a way of disrupting the services. That might be fun.

Then Chalmers went into Archie MacNicoll's shop. MacNicoll promptly asked him to come to a service. He was very insistent and, rather to his own surprise, Chalmers agreed to go. And go he did, although it was a night of rain. The service was being held in a joiner's loft and, as he climbed the stairs, Chalmers was struck by the singing. He had never heard the hundredth Psalm sung like this. The first evangelist then spoke to Revelation 22:17 and those words 'seemed to speak directly to me'. Chalmers left the meeting excited and confused, unable to give a coherent report to MacNicoll.

The change begun in the joiner's loft continued the next Sunday in the Free Church, where he came under a crushing sense of sin, and then reached completion the following Monday as he talked things over with the United Presbyterian minister. The minister led Chalmers to the promises of salvation and he was able to say that a new gladness came into his heart.

It was then that he remembered the promise made years before. James Chalmers knew that the time had come. His preparation for the mission field was suitably arduous and, as we have seen, he went out to serve his Master with his courage high.

The natives had their own name for Chalmers, Tamate, which was the nearest they could get to pronouncing the Scottish surname. Chalmers used his new name with pride, feeling that it brought him closer to the people he had come to love. There is no doubt that they loved him, and if he was a hero in Scotland, he was an apostle and saint in New Guinea. When the great adventure that had begun in a joiner's loft came to its end on a remote South Sea Island, one of his native teachers wrote to the mission leader, 'Hear my wish. It is a great wish. The remainder of my strength I would spend in the place where Tamate and Mr Tomkins were killed. In that village I would live. In that place where they killed men, Jesus Christ's name and his word I would teach to the people, that they may become Jesus' children.'

Index